Building a Clinic in Africa

Tales of Beans, Bats, and a Dream

Patricia Nau Mertz

Patricia Nau Mertz

Building a Clinic in Africa
Tales of Beans, Bats and a Dream

Published by BooxAi

ISBN: 978-965-578-084-0

This book is dedicated not only to Chas and Kevin who have aided me in times of need, but everyone who has ever supported Ivory Coast Mothers and Children (<u>www.IvoryCoastAid.org</u>).

Thank you. Your kindness has touched me and so many more.

It was nearing 10 PM, as I was settling into my cozy bed with an old yellowed, musty, smelling Jane Austen book, and out came the same screeching heavy metal audio tape from across the way that would play on a continuous loop until almost daybreak.

* * *

"I am losing it!" "I... am... losing it!"

I tossed and turned. Never a fan of loud, heavy metal American rock music with its distorted, aggressive electric guitar melodies, but when combined with a techno-West African-disco interpretation all day, at full volume, on bad speakers until after 2 AM, it was pure torture.

The bangi bar that didn't have a name owned only 3 audio tapes to play on their off-brand boom box. The proud new owners started playing the same tunes sometimes as early as 7:30 AM. Their very limited playlist began with a popular upbeat Ivorian medley that was classic, followed by a Bob Marley hit, "This is my message to you... Everything's gonna be alright." I hung on to the reggae message with deep conviction because I needed to believe that one day, everything would be alright.

"Why couldn't they just play more Bob Marley or even more old Ivorian songs?" I groaned to myself. "And turn the damn thing down!"

My patience had run out. I had reached my limit. I lost it. The worst of the worst heavy metal songs was painfully piercing my frontal lobes once again, and I could not restrain myself for one more second. I burst out from under my green tucked-in mosquito net. In my bedhead, nightgown, and flip-flops, I stomped across the room and slammed open the front door. At that moment, I was face to face with a giant python that was coiled up on the concrete ledge of the front steps, and then I looked directly into his eyes and said, "You, mother-fucker, are just going to have to wait a minute."

I stormed across the way towards the drunk men gathered on the long benches with their oversized speakers and cups made from a coconut filled with bangi to kindly ask them how long they were planning on carrying on. One of them dismissed me by blurting out, "When we run out of bangi, of course." I could hear the snickering in the background.

They were startled to see the sight of me, it was clear, and they did not want to hear any of my complaints to interrupt their soirée. I am fully aware that nobody wants to hear a command to put an end to a good party. I know. I am sometimes lovingly referred to as "Party Pat", but not in Africa. It was obvious, I was a persona non grata. I swiftly turned around and marched back towards my house, and then screamed at the top of my lungs for all to hear the battle cry, "Seeeer pent! Serpent!"

Within 45 seconds, my courtyard was overrun with men and boys fully equipped with their weapons of large sticks and stones. They beat the python to a pulp.

"Overkill! That's what is meant by overkill." The snake represents everything evil and is the unwelcome devil to the villagers. It was a grand victory for me that there was no more of their music that night, and in fact, they never again met outside my bedroom window, thanks to an exaggerated story I told the chief of the village the following day. I let him know about my invitation to live in a neighboring village where there is peace and quiet.

"Patricia, viens habiter chez nous," Come and live with us, I remembered someone half-jokingly say to me during a casual conversation.

It was true that I was invited to live in another village, but it was never a formal invitation by any means. Frankly, I didn't care how it happened. I told the chief, and the outcome was that the very next

2

night, he ordered the revelers to move their business away from me to the other end of the small rural village.

"Merci beaucoup, Chef!"

What a relief it was to snuggle in my bed once again with my old, borrowed book, and with a renewed sense of calm.

When the group of young men initially played their music early one evening to launch their new bangi business, I dropped in to congratulate them and to wish them luck. Crudely made benches formed a big square around a pair of mega speakers that drowned out any attempt for conversation. The bar was made of bamboo sticks and palm fronds for the roof gathered from the surrounding bamboo forest. The men were anxious to share a glass of their milky-looking palm wine poured into a rounded wood-like cup. They grinned from ear to ear about the possibilities of making some money in the impoverished village.

The day after my neighborly visit to the bangi bar, the pious elderly chief of the village called me over to his house through one of his lackeys.

"Mme. Patricia, Il ne faut pas y aller!" He made it very clear to me that I was never allowed to go there again. "You are a woman, and you are sending out the wrong message to the community." He gave me an order.

Why would my having a drink with some young men be outlawed? This is not good, I thought. How was I going to adapt to such an antiquated culture? I had many doubts that I would ever adjust to their norms. And how was I supposed to get to know the men? Since the chief was the last word, I agreed to follow his command, at least in the village. After all, I was their guest as a Peace Corps volunteer. Their rules and their lives were much different than living in downtown Chicago.

Changes

Something wasn't right with me. A wave of restless anxiety was controlling my morning. It was my day off work as I sat at the counter in my recently remodeled "Euro" kitchen with views down Astor, a beautiful tree-lined street in the Gold Coast near the lake. I was itching for something, and I didn't know what. I had a plum job, planning dinners and outings for the pampered employees and clients at Goldman Sachs, and making the most money ever with lots of perks, even though some of the prima-donnas were often difficult to impress. I started thinking how my work routine was always in search of "the best," "the finest," "and "perfect" because for an event planner or a concierge, that is the job description. I continually reminded myself of the credo to always "go above and beyond and to exceed expectations". But I wondered how anything could really ever be good enough for them.

Perusing the local newspaper "The Reader" out of boredom, I spotted an ad that said, "The toughest job you'll ever love. Join the Peace Corps." The sentence hit me on the head like a hammer, along with the sudden realization that I could finally do whatever I wanted in my life and maybe find work that would be more worthwhile.

Long time divorced, I had recently lost both of my beloved parents after long illnesses. My sons, Mike and Matt, in their 20s, had graduated from the university, were employed in the city, living on their own, and fully immersed in their new exciting young lives. At that very moment, I dialed the number of the Peace Corps Chicago office and set up an interview scheduled for the next day.

"Is there anything you need to know right now that would help you decide if the Peace Corps would be the right choice for you?" the Chicago manager inquired as I sat squirming on the chair facing him.

I meekly responded, "I would really need water."

He didn't flinch, "Yes, uh huh, we all need water."

Since that was probably one of the dumbest responses he had ever heard in an interview, I was sure that I had blown any chance of them ever calling me back. To my surprise, my acceptance letter arrived a few months later, but it said that I needed to wait a full year because I was still grieving my father's death. I was overjoyed at the prospect of a real adventure of consequence and was bubbling over to tell the world, or at least my close friends and family.

"What??? You are 55 years old! You have never even been camping before, and you want to live in a developing country for 2 years and 3 months? In Sub-Saharan Africa? Are you crazy?"

Similar remarks were coming in from every corner. Most did not believe that I was serious and regarded the idea as one of my pipe dreams because I was "accustomed to the comforts of life." Since both of my sons also have a sense of adventure, I was relieved that my Peace Corps idea, at least, appealed to them.

If it was true that I was a "late bloomer," as it was said of me over 35 years ago in my Delta Gamma pledge class, then I had some serious blooming and growing to do, I decided. I wanted a challenge to ignite my soul and shake up my being. I felt a sense of urgency.

The big departure day was drawing near. There was an inch-thick booklet sent to me from the Peace Corps office in Washington that had been staring me in the face for over three months and was to be read in full before my journey.

On a sunny Saturday morning, feeling the pressure to complete the task, I walked over to my favorite outdoor corner coffee shop to hunker down and dig into the details about what the future would hold for me. I was making good progress flipping through the pages until I came upon the chapter "Safety and Security" when a majestic red-orange and black Monarch butterfly fluttered over and landed at the top of the page on those exact written words, "Safety and Security".

My eyes filled with tears, recalling one of my mother's favorite refrains to me, "Patsy, keep your wits about you." I have a propensity for mind wandering, day dreaming and bumping into things, I admit.

When the message fully resonated, the butterfly flew away. I received the warning loud and clear and left the café with a strong sense of foreboding.

There was a long to-do list glaring at me that included, "Find a renter for my condo, pack it up for rental, take its contents to a storage unit, pack a suitcase with the suggested outdoor lifestyle-type items including modest looking long skirts, go shopping (I owned no clothing fitting their descriptions and never owned a backpack or water bottle)." I had already given my 2 weeks' notice and felt paralyzed at the thought of what seemed like herculean tasks ahead.

I could not call any friends or family because I pretended to have everything under control and wanted to avoid hearing any more negative comments. My solution was to call my childhood friend, Sara, who always responded in a calm manner whenever I was frazzled.

"Help! I need to talk this through."

She listened and surprised me by almost immediately packing her bag and flying halfway across the country, leaving her flourishing toy and gift shop in Maine to help me attack the dreaded list. She rented a 4x4 at the airport and drove around to help run errands. We packed boxes along with countless other tasks while I made up the piles for trash, storage and donations. We worked together tirelessly into the wee hours, checking off the list with music blaring and making it fun like we always did since we were kids jumping on the beds.

The truth was that I was terrified to go to Africa and to leave the luxury and comfort of my home and my classy job at Goldman. I was brimming with self-doubt regarding my knowledge of French, fears about my bad, delicate stomach, and my general ability to succeed in my work as a volunteer with all the young 20-something over-achievers.

My designer friend said that I would be sleeping with snakes under my bed, which gave me nightmares and brought up scary childhood memories of how my older sister tormented me about snakes lurking on the bedroom floor, always in a ready position to bite my feet off. I was afraid of the unknown, but I had resolved to go and embrace my fear, my insecurities, and the idea of snakes. Most importantly, I resolved to keep "my wits about me."

I was born on Eleanor Roosevelt's birthday, October 11. Eleanor's words, "You gain strength, courage, and confidence by every experience in which you stop to look fear in the face." The anxiety that I was experiencing was part of the process, and I kept her wise words close to me.

My sons and family threw me the most memorable going away party that I could ever imagine at my son, Michael's townhouse. It was rowdy and wild, with music playing on all three floors, full-tilt skits poking good fun at me, and a medley of songs and guitars from the talented cousins.

When the Chicago Police came knocking on the door responding to the neighbors' complaints, I invited them in and gave them a tour of his place. To my amazement, a while later, they were still there hanging out on the couches, chatting up the crowd.

It rained in torrents that night, but it did not stop the many merry-makers from coming out to say goodbye. I finally felt the votes of confidence from my family and friends that I wanted and needed. The party was the perfect tonic. As my mother used to say when something was wonderful, "Lock it in your heart."

The evening before I left, my younger brother Nick, my all-time favorite childhood, adventurous playmate, took me out for dinner and the movie, "Moulin Rouge" which became my favorite film. I was, at last, bursting at the seams with anticipation and finally ready for the unknown.

After the exhausting plane ride to the Ivory Coast via a night in Philadelphia with the new volunteers, and a week of non-stop cultural indoctrination meetings at a farm for nuns outside the capital city, Abidjan, I was relieved to finally be alone. I shut my bedroom door with my new host family who warmly welcomed me to begin our three months of training in Alépé. I collapsed on my thin foam mattress, feeling the wooden planks below in the scrubbed-clean room. The walls were painted Smurf blue many years before but were dismally stained from wear. It was furnished with one straight wooden chair and a simple matching table placed under the window with bars on it looking out at another concrete dwelling. During those first quiet moments alone, I wallowed in more self-doubt and spilled a bucket of tears into my pillow but immediately composed myself when I heard a knock on the door.

Madame called my name, "Pa tree see a viens." I was told to come out because someone was there bearing a gift.

Ok, "Tout de suite."

I wiped off my face, practiced a smile, and obediently went to the main room where the whole family had gathered. Standing outside the front door was a kind-looking elderly man with a dirty well-worn grey cloth bag slung over his shoulder. I had trouble understanding what he was saying. He stepped inside and dumped the contents of his bag on the floor in front of me. It was loaded with six giant, flattened, dead rat-like creatures called agouti, their most desired bush meat.

"Noooo!" I cried since I fear rats and had never seen or heard of agouti before, dead or alive. Oops, I must have missed that part of the food presentation at the nunnery when we arrived for the indoctrination. Flight was my only reaction. I escaped to my room and shut the door amid a chorus of laughter.

8

"Oh my God, I will never make it here," I moaned while trying to erase the disturbing image ingrained in my mind.

I was not polite in refusing his gift. I was admonished and later apologized to the family.

During that same first night, I woke up looking for the bathroom with my flashlight and was startled to see my new family in the main room on the floor laid out in rows sleeping on their mats. I didn't realize that it was the norm to sleep on the floor, and to think that I was hogging up a whole room!

We all arrived in the bustling town of Côte d'Ivoire, West Africa, ready for classes on health, safety, language, customs, traditions, and in my selected work, education. I slowly began to assimilate into my host family, the group of twenty exuberant and exceptional young volunteers, and the enthusiastic and brilliant Ivorian, English-speaking trainers.

It was hot and humid at the bustling market on the way to class. My senses were assaulted with smells of earthiness, spiced foods, and wood smoke. There were mounds of charcoal being sold everywhere for the women to cook their food, along with an array of unfamiliar, unpackaged spices and mounds of colorful vegetables. There were curious sounds of chattering of women wearing vibrant colors in unfamiliar patterns speaking loudly as they bartered in a strange language.

Chinese cheap housewares and tools brought in from the capital were set up on stands next to piles of bright-colored fabrics neatly folded called "pagne" that were the staple used for everything from clothing to diapers. The raw meat, which was available to those who could afford it, was hanging in full view with hungry flies feverishly buzzing around. Roaming goats, sheep, and dogs shared the sunken, cracked, and broken sidewalks. I quickly learned to keep my eyes fixed on the ground to avoid piles of excrement left by the wandering animals and avoid stubbing my sandaled toe on the crumbling ground while taking it all in.

The first time I walked to class, I crossed paths with a baby chicken. There was hell to pay for that misstep, when the mother appeared, and began attacking me with her angry beak. I was grateful that a young child had accompanied me and warded her off.

The night before, a goat gave birth outside my window. I hurled myself out of bed after hearing all the commotion to see a newborn baby goat screaming and jump-dancing around with the cord still on it. The mother just stared at it. So, needless to say, I was a bit jittery.

I settled into my unfamiliar surroundings with full-blown menopause, complete with night sweats and mood swings, strange skin rashes, and accelerated digestion problems, along with the oversized bugs, the towering vegetation, and the very kind people. Everything was new which called for major adjustments in my psyche. It was over-whelming and transformative. I thought that I might just have to slow down a bit which forced me to be in the moment.

To begin each day during the training, the lively volunteers shared their own personal experiences in adapting to the new culture with their assigned families. The process became a type of group therapy for support and encouragement. We all had a tale or two to tell during training.

One volunteer, Mike, quipped, "I think I ate the cat for dinner last night."

Another young woman, Laura, arrived crying almost every day out of control, "I just can't cope with anything! I want to get out of here!" She wound up staying and learned French and flourished.

A couple of other people left for home in the States before I ever knew their names.

One of my "shares" was that I was highly anticipating my first green salad after living there for almost two months, but discovered that everyone's idea of a salad is not quite the same as my own. Madame was preparing my evening meal as I sat on a low stool outside to watch her while taking the opportunity to practice my French in conversation with her. Sitting near the open fire also on a low stool, she skillfully wielded a large machete-type knife and peeled the cucumber and carrots in her hand without a cutting board. Afterward, she carefully washed the delicate fresh lettuce in a bucket filled with a bleach/water solution. I learned that she and other host mothers were trained to prepare food hygienically for the American guest volunteers to help prevent illnesses.

I could hear the sizzling oil in a big black pot on the fire, and I assumed that it was for a meal for her come-and-go ne'er-do-well husband. I had already stood up to retreat towards the dinner table at her suggestion when I looked over my shoulder. Madame began pouring the entire contents of the pot of boiling oil that was filled with kidneys from I don't know what kind of animal, over my beautiful, formerly crisp, fresh, green garden salad.

"Noooooooo," I couldn't suppress my disappointment.

Madame woke up at 3 AM most mornings to carry her *attiéké* that she spent days preparing by peeling the tough skin from the cassava (*manioc*), grating, cooking, and fermenting it, bagging it, and then traveling hours to the market in Abidjan and finally, selling it for less than fifty cents. She never stopped working like most of the other women I met. I grew to respect her work ethic and how she lovingly and cheerfully cared for her young children, and for me.

She fed her husband first when he was home along with any other male guest. The children were in the next round. And then she sat with me to eat her meal. It was the only time I ever saw her when she wasn't preparing, cleaning, caring for the children or working on her *attiéké*. She wanted to know about my family and about my life and I wanted to hear about her. How I struggled to understand the African French!

After three months of training 5-1/2 long days a week was completed, we were finally prepared to meet the people in our newly assigned

11

villages and begin our work. Our wonderful Peace Corps Country Director, Marty, had a highly trained staff who matched each one of us with a new site that would fit the needs and requests of both the village and the volunteer. We were all anxious to live on our own and find out where each one of us would be located.

The announcements were read during a ceremony when we all dressed in African garb and were individually given a small piece of paper with the population and village description, including information on where to find the closest market. I had expressed a desire for an indoor toilet because of my own personal issues. When the news broke that I received one, everybody cheered because while training, the volunteers heard my continual complaints about my never-ending stomach challenges.

It was announced officially, "Patricia to Braffouéby!"

Braffouéby

I smiled the moment I walked in to see my own freshly painted, still-wet Smurf-blue-colored house where I would live for the next two years. It was, in fact, the only color of paint available besides white. I was pleased that they made such an effort for me, but puzzled as to why they asked me what color I wanted the rooms to be painted. My ill-considered response was "butter yellow."

My large and fine cement house was in the oldest and busiest part of the village on the main road, with clean cement floors, a separate bedroom, a kitchen area, and a toilet. I was warned that the water rarely came out of the faucet, and we were instructed to boil and filter whatever water we drank, whether from the well or the sink. Electricity worked on some days.

For the bucket baths and flushing and drinking, Odette, my dear neighbor, delivered a fresh pail of water from the well every day to my door in case the faucet was dry. We were all given a large contraption that double filtered the water to prevent worms. I had water, as promised, and I treasured the electricity. I learned to use the light judicially because of the flurry of bugs that were instantly attracted to the light.

Odette's husband descended from one of the five founding families of the village, Ablo Bosso, and the family owned the house where I was staying. Félix Houphouët-Boigny himself slept in the same house for a couple of nights in the 1980s. He was the first President of the Ivory Coast, where he ruled for twenty years. He gifted the impoverished village of Braffouéby with electricity as an expression of his gratitude, but hardly anyone could afford to buy kerosene for their lamps, much less pay an expensive bill for electricity.

My favorite place was an elevated little patio outside the door with enough room for chairs and a table and a view of our spacious horseshoe-shaped courtyard. There was one old hut that faced a house on the other side made of cement bricks that belonged to Odette and her husband. They also have a large open-air shelter used as a traditional outside kitchen made of bamboo sticks and a palm-leaf thatched roof. Wooden chairs and benches were lined up around her area where she builds fires to cook meals and make her *attiéké* for sale. It is also used as the place where her friends stop in to chat and help her out with the work. Like the other women in the village, I would hear the daily sounds of her pounding the cassava with a giant mortar and pestle to prepare *foutou*, the traditional mid-day favorite.

Figure 1 Making attiéke

13

Figure 2 My New Handmade Furniture

Figure 3 A cup of bangi palm wine in a coconut cup

A graceful giant Ficus tree with spectacular, glossy, green leaves stood next to my house like an expansive umbrella to give much-needed shade. It was rare to have a tree around a house because the community used their machetes to keep vegetation cut low to prevent the dreaded snakes. It was a stunning tree and one of my favorite things about the village and my home. I was crushed to learn that they cut it down years later.

"Pourquoi?" I asked why already knowing the answer.

"Serpents!" the neighbor said with a snarl shaking her head.

Next to my house lived a very old woman in a square hut made of natural materials, bamboo sticks, and mud. She had to be in her 80s and in very frail health. It was dark inside, where her belongings were stacked neatly along the walls, and her sleeping mat rolled up near the door. Her family lived elsewhere, which was unusual because families, as a rule, lived together. I never understood much about her. After she passed away years later, the hut collapsed into a heap of debris and remained there for years like a monument to her memory.

"Patricia, attention!" my neighbor, Odette, warned me one afternoon during my first weeks in the village.

"Look over there! She is the witch who cast a spell on the man who just died across the way from you. Stay away from her!"

Sorcery was intertwined in almost every story about health, death, or wealth. People don't openly speak of it to me anymore like they did 20 years ago, but it will forever be at the base of their culture. If someone was sick, the family member would blame the person who they believed cast the evil spell. There was little interest in finding out how someone had died or what kind of illness they had since most never went to a hospital to receive a professional diagnosis. Being sick was often a death sentence. Science didn't seem to exist. I remember inquiring about the cause of death multiple times because of the numerous funerals that I attended of people young and old.

I was usually warned, "It doesn't matter how the person died. The fact remains, he is dead!" I was instructed instead to ask, "Who do you think cast the fateful spell?"

The toll from extreme poverty and corruption is heartbreaking because it affects people's futures. 75% of Ivorian rural women live below the poverty line. Poor health and education, along with the continued lack of economic development, hampers the future of the children. Malnutrition and anemia weaken them from learning at school and eventually being able to work. All these factors and more perpetuate the cycle of poverty.

"How will I ever be able to make my mark here when I don't know where to start, much less communicate with anyone? Do I have what it takes? I can't do this. How do I begin? Is it too late to leave? I need to find a way." I began to spiral into a deep despair. Writing letters was my therapy. Reading was my escape.

One morning little Beatrice knocked on my door, and with her big winning smile, she said, "Bonjour, Madame."

At first, the young children would only observe me from afar, but one by one, they became my new best friends, my sweetest light, and my source of joy. They eagerly shared with me their hopes and dreams which I always encouraged them to do. I had friends!

On my first day working in the schools, I left early in the morning to meet my supervisor at a nearby school. He revealed he had just started his new position.

"Bienvenue, Patricia!" He warmly welcomed me and then began, "The former director was recently given a large sum of money from the government to repair some of the dilapidated schools with dirt floors, leaking roofs, and broken desks. The money has disappeared, and so has he. I am now your new Director."

The sum must have been too much temptation for him since he probably never saw or held that much money in his hands at one time. He absconded with all of it. He left his job and his family and his village, and he was nowhere to be found. He ruined his name forever and would never again be able to return home.

After hearing the dreadful news, my new Director gave me my assignment, which was to travel to five different villages for a total of 11 schools, and asked me to report to him every Friday with my lesson plans and description of my progress at each of them. Somehow, I was under the impression that I would work at the school in my assigned village of Braffouéby and not be spread quite so thinly. The task was daunting. I didn't know my way around, and I have a knack for getting lost because of my poor sense of direction. The rural red dirt roads are lined with bamboo and palm trees, and all looked the same to me. With no street names or addresses, at first, I struggled to meet the challenges.

None of the schools had working toilets. Sometimes I would be caught somewhere walking along a wretched road through the thick forests with no place to hide during a monsoon rain en route to the next village or find myself struggling to make it home before my lower intestine exploded.

To add a another layer to my insecurities, African French mixed with their local language is not the same as the French I learned in college or in training, and there were a multitude of elders, parents, teachers, and children in each village to keep straight with all of their cultural idiosyncrasies. My mantra became, "Do my best, be prepared, and show up."

The undeveloped infrastructure was alarming. The narrow rough red clay roads surrounding the villages were treacherous, and I hardly ever saw any cars traveling on them. And when I did, I would often see men and boys gathered to push some car out of a rut. Some of the holes in the roads were so deep that people would fill them with rags so that a possible car could pass over or be pushed out of the rut. The scenario reminded me of some crazy video game that my sons played. A rare driver or taxi was forced to turn the steering wheel sharply in one direction and then abruptly in the other direction to avoid the trenches.

To arrive at two of the villages, both Bacanou A and Bacanou B, I caught a ride on the back of a truck in another village, Bécedi. It was always a crap shoot if I made it in time or not. Getting back was even more challenging since there was so little traffic out there. The people, however, always made it worth my while because they were so gracious in offering me a place to stay, dinner and a Fanta. However, after a long day, I much more preferred to get back to Braffouéby.

Early one morning before school, I experienced fifteen minutes of terror as I attempted the commute on my new Trek bike that was gifted by the Peace Corps. Trying my best to swerve along the crater-filled dirt road, ignoring my trembling hands while balancing on the skinny tires, I became so tense and frightened that I had second thoughts, and I finally came to my senses.

"Nope, not for me!" I turned around, brought it back, and never rode the bike again.

The children, however, never gave up, begging me for a turn to ride it. Too bad they spotted it, but I knew the bike would have caused too much bickering and too many disagreements over whose turn it was. From that day on, I charged forward on foot over the rough terrain to the faraway schools since there was not really a choice, and I needed to arrive in one piece. I continued to show up out of breath and drenched in perspiration and sometimes rain often wondering if my short hair would ever dry.

The Peace Corps office in Abidjan had loads of material for students containing information for the girls' and boys' clubs that I decided to organize. It was a minimum of a one-and-a-half-hour bus ride away, depending on the route. Some busses would veer off the main road into the different villages to load up the tired and eager passengers who sought to earn enough money in the larger markets to feed their families. They would board the bus burdened with a variety of giant wrapped bundles ready for sale at the market, sometimes tying their load on top of the bus. A live animal strapped on the top would slow down the trip exponentially. I was routinely bewildered when I would catch one of the indirect routes since the busses operate on a loose alternating schedule, whatever that meant. One rule was in stone. If it was a direct route, the bus would never leave the station until it was full, which meant the trip entailed a lot of waiting.

Occasionally, the bus would make stops along the highway, allowing passengers to find a makeshift restroom in the nearby bushes. I vividly recall an incident where someone unintentionally tracked in a foul-smelling substance on their sandals, which served as a valuable lesson for me to never leave my backpack on the floor near the aisle. A very kind observant woman on board noticed what had happened, and then she quickly cleaned it off for me. I bought a new no-name backpack at the market that very same day which suited me just fine.

If ever there existed a hell on earth, it was Adjamé, the bus station and market in Abidjan. It was teaming with scores of poverty-stricken children peddling whatever they could get their hands on. Why weren't they in school? It was a hustle, chaotic and gritty, and I could usually count on a tussle over someone wanting to carry my backpack for me. Everyone was desperate to sell something everywhere I looked.

Once while I was getting off the bus, an older street kid grabbed at my bag, wanting to "help carry" it for me, but I hung on to it for dear life. He punched me in the stomach and ran away. The three women who witnessed the incident were outraged. One of them comforted me, while the other two darted after the kid. I didn't stay around to see if they caught him because when I spotted a taxi, I got the hell out of there. I was used to having someone pester me to carry the backpack, but I never associated it with any kind of violence. Once again, a woman stepped up to rectify a situation.

I witnessed many children working and discriminated against in the markets carrying heavy loads knowing they are without proper food, healthcare, and most likely, without a registered birth certificate to have access to education, healthcare, and social services. Without proper identification these individuals are often excluded and are at a higher possibility of experiencing exploitation, discrimination, and abuse.

Since 2012 there has been a national plan and policy for the protection of children to fight against child abuse and child labor. The Ivory Coast produces about 45% of the global supply of cocoa. Unfortunately, in 2021 up north in the giant cocoa fields, United States chocolate corporations were accused of child slavery, low pay, rights abuses, and structural poverty against thousands of minors. The children were fed and paid little, they worked long hours, and were isolated from other child workers. In the village where I lived,

19

parents made use of young children for help at home and in the fields.

Figure 4 Child with a machete in the forest

During one of my early errands in the deteriorating, but once grand capital city of Abidjan, I unexpectedly bumped into a friend at the Peace Corps office. After I gathered some material for my school clubs, we both went down the street to visit a little place that sold the most delicious samosas I ever tasted.

"The sky has turned pitch black! Looks like a big storm is coming in," I remarked.

"No," she said. "Those are bats. And you need to watch where you are walking!"

She had already honed her navigation skills along the hazardous sidewalks while I was tripping and hopping like a klutz along beside her. My next thought was, "Snakes… and bats and rats…how nice." I am happy now that I didn't know about the dangers of bat guano droppings carrying pathogens since there were enough warnings out there for us already about every other darn thing.

The teachers in the schools had no books, paper, and usually no chalk. I noticed teachers and students licking their fingers to write on the chalkboards and on their mini green boards because they lacked basic school supplies. I thought printed material for the clubs would be valuable so that the teachers would have a reference to keep, and the Peace Corps office had plenty of documents for us to use. I went on several more missions to obtain the needed printed information about sex, HIV/AIDS, and the environment but soon I was surprised to find a sign taped to the Xerox machine that read, "Do not use this copier without permission." I thought, mmmmm, the sign was perhaps most likely directed at me.

The students were timid and not accustomed to having class discussions because their way of learning was through repetition. The children's classroom lives were regimented under authoritarian school rules, and the kids knew they would suffer corporal punishment if they misbehaved, even though it had been outlawed. Many children were truant and hiding out during the day for fear of being beaten, according to the children I talked to. One spunky little girl from a very large family who lived close to me was often truant because she said the teacher beat her. I would often take her hand and march her back to school, but it didn't do much good. She "married" at age 13 and now has five children with no father present.

"Take my hand, Rose. It's time to go to school if you want your dreams to come true."

Little did I know, that would be a long shot.

During a club session for the girls, while we were discussing, but mainly, I was talking about the importance of them understanding consent and practicing assertiveness. A sudden downpour, monsoon style, interrupted our class. As the rain pounded relentlessly on the tin roof of the classroom, the sound became magnified just as I was having them practice saying the word "non" out loud. I was inspired by Jesse Jackson's empowering poem "I Am Somebody." His resounding words came to me with the messages of self-respect, self-care, and the importance of self-protection. They had never heard of Jesse Jackson, of course, but we continued to yell the word "non" at the tops of our lungs in competition with the deafening sounds from above. We yelled so loudly that it ultimately triggered spontaneous laughter. I hoped to send the message, "Say no" and "Don't give up your dreams by having sex on the lame promise of a cheap gift". The

21

girls relaxed when the rain subsided, and I was relieved that we could finally hear ourselves talk. Then the water began pouring in on one side of the classroom onto the hard clay floor. I could only think of the greedy Director guy who disappeared with the cash and how they could have had that roof repaired for the teachers, the students, and for me.

Braffouéby had the only clean-up campaign that I ever noticed. The young boys' group celebrated "Clean-up Day" after a secret ceremony, signifying their transition into manhood. As part of their initiation, the group had the task of raking up trash in the village. Most people buried their trash to avoid littering, but some had little regard for the burying rule.

There wasn't much of an effort to build latrines because of a lack of funding, and open defecation was, therefore, the norm. "Pas d'argent, Pas de moyen" was the excuse, "no money."

Human waste can easily seep into rivers or groundwater contaminating them with harmful bacteria, parasites and viruses which can lead to the spread of waterborne diseases like cholera, typhoid, and diarrhea which are preventable diseases. The lack of sanitation facilities in the entire village continues to be a big risk to the community and especially for women and girls. Open defecation with the lack of privacy and dignity have negative psychological effects on the individuals. Additionally, the practice hampers socio-economic development and impacts their productivity.

The children quarreled over who would get to take out my trash. I would see them walking past my window carrying post-cards, zip lock bags, an empty vitamin bottle or when little Frank found an empty cereal box, he proudly wore it on his head. They were supposed to dig a hole and bury it, but unfortunately, it didn't bother me enough to take out my own garbage. I just didn't go there. It must have been an old division of duties rule that I clung to from growing up. Most importantly, I knew people used the weeds as toilets and also for burying their garbage, I didn't want to make a mistake and dig around anywhere near there. The kids knew the territory.

"Don't drop your discarded paper or those awful white plastic bags on the ground," I instructed a boy's club and then feebly attempted to tell them the impactful story of the old "Indian with the Tear" commercial from the States in 1971. I began with, "The Indians were the first people to live in America. The Indian chief was looking out over his land that was once pristine and is now covered in garbage." I continued the narrative with how my own generation was inspired by the Indian and for us to be conscious of creating a cleaner, more litter-free environment. I am not sure the Indian message translated very well or resonated fully or even a little bit with the students, but anyway, the boys were attentive while I told them the story which, by the way, triggered one of my own tears too.

The Day That Changed the World

There was a knock on my door late one Saturday morning. It was Jacques, the well-behaved young son of the chief, coming over to warn me that the chief and two other men were on their way over to meet with me.

"Something was up," I thought because it was not a usual occurrence for the Chief to come to my place to pay me a visit. Normally, I would be commissioned to go to his place.

I was familiar with the drill whenever I had adult visitors. I moved my newly purchased handmade wooden chairs outside to the patio and the small matching table crafted by the same local carpenter to place the water that I would offer my guests. The tall, very thin dignified chief was in ceremonial garb, a floor-length, embroidered with gold threads boubou made from a muted colored *pagne*. His ever-present aide and, oddly enough, two Japanese businessmen were alongside him. The two men happened to be doing business not too far away in Elibou, a bustling village along the highway with a busy market scene.

While they were there, they learned that there was an American living nearby and were aware of the local protocol of first visiting the chief upon entering a village.

After my guests were seated and we finished the formalities which included introductions, offering the traditional glass of water, and inquiries about the family, I then asked the perfunctory question, "What is the news of the day?"

One of the Japanese men solemnly delivered the headline story about the New York City Twin Towers. They regretted that they did not have any more details but that it was called "a terrorist attack." All I could think about was contacting my sons. I knew there were no phones or computers available anywhere around that I could use that afternoon but there were phones in Dabou and Abidjan, a bus ride away.

Early the next morning, I set off to Sikensi to board a bus going to either one of the cities, Dabou or Abidjan. Whichever bus left the station first, I would be on it. The next bus was headed to Dabou, where I had never been, but I was relieved that it was closer than Abidjan, and I figured it would be a much easier place to navigate. After the long, anxious bus ride, I was let off at the end of the line stop located in mid-town. I walked up and down the gravel road entering every shop and shack along the way and randomly asking anyone I saw if they knew where I could find a telephone. An elderly man standing in front of his ramshackle store invited me inside and led me to the messy back corner of the room. There was a ray of sunlight filtering in from the front, and a stool next to an old dusty black telephone on a table, where I called my eldest son, Michael.

He kept repeating the same words, "Mom, you have no idea."

He was right that I did not have any idea about what had happened five long days ago.

He continued, "People are dead, the Board of Trade is closed, and there are no planes flying."

Mike assured me that he and Matt were safe, but I was interrupted and instructed to hang up quickly as the nice shopkeeper was soon leaning heavily on me to make haste.

I was dazed and shaken like most of the world, I learned later. I began wandering aimlessly down that same road until I came upon a tidy little restaurant with nobody in it and then stumbled inside. I pulled up a faded-looking outdoor molded plastic chair at a paint-chipped table to sit down when a captivating middle-aged woman approached me wearing a very high coal-black colored Marge Simpson-styled wig. She looked serene and wore loads of different shades of eyeshadow with heavy long curly false eyelashes. She was resplendent in a shapely green and yellow colored long dress that fit her curves just right. She emanated kindness, tenderness, and love. I was instantly enthralled by her mystical qualities, and I was under her spell. The gracious woman sensed the tragedy that had happened because she comforted me soon after I was seated and then I broke down and cried.

"Do you want to eat some roast chicken?" she asked.

"Oui!" I responded without hesitation, even though I wasn't hungry.

Roast chicken was a luxury and never made me sick. Madame went to the back of the restaurant somewhere outside to find a bird to kill, pluck and roast on an outdoor fire. I was there for hours as she prepared the meal while checking in on me regularly to sit by my side to assure me that there would one day be peace. I had never experienced anyone like her before. She was like an apparition, unreal and at the same time very comforting.

How could she be so sure that life would go on, I thought, when neither of us knew anything about what had really occurred that day.

On my way back to the bus station, I happened upon a newsstand with a haunting blurry-looking photo of the burning buildings on the front page of the newspaper with very little other information.

A week later, I was at home making my coffee early on Sunday morning when I looked out the kitchen window to see a few young girls all dressed up in their finest clothes walking intently towards my door with the message that I should go to church. Since the girls came over expressly to invite me to mass, I replied that I would attend, but I knew I would be a little late because I was still lingering over my coffee.

When I eventually made my way to an empty pew in the back of the church, many parishioners turned around to gape at me, which felt strange and uncomfortable. Most of them were familiar with me by then, except for the little babies who would catch sight of my blonde hair and white skin and then belt out a horrific scream until they could safely bury their heads in their mothers' arms. It was uplifting to join the congregation who were singing and dancing up and down the aisles and around the church while the women waved and flipped their white handkerchiefs in time to the rhythmic hymns.

At the end of the service, the priest began the exit procession down the middle aisle, and the multitudes made their way in turn out the door behind him. I followed their lead, and before I knew it, there was a large crowd gathered around me. One of the women exclaimed that they were going to walk me home. They kept the circle around me, and began a serenade and a dance-walk through the village to my courtyard, where we rallied under the giant Ficus tree that embraced us all like a living, loving, protective hug. As the crowd moved their bodies to the beat of the joyful songs, the priest followed with a prayer thanking God for all our blessings. One of the women spoke kind words for those who had lost their lives during the unspeakable tragedy, and another man recited more prayers. The women put their arms around me and expressed their sadness about the suffering in my country. For the first time, I felt that I was not alone in the village, and I believed that I was truly in a place where I should be. That Sunday morning, I reaffirmed the promise I had made to myself that I would do my best for the people in Braffouéby every day while I was living there. My emotions were on a rollercoaster ride.

Les Enfants

On the next Saturday morning, I noticed that there were some hard-boiled eggs missing from the windowsill that I had set out earlier to cool. I asked around to the children who were playing outside my door.

"Ok, les enfants, who knows where the eggs are?"

It was not the first time that something had disappeared from my place, and I was annoyed.

They immediately put the blame on frail little Agnes, who lived a few courtyards over.

"C'est Agnes! C'est Agnes!"

I told them, "I will speak to Agnes the next time she comes by."

"Non, Maintenant!" The children kept urging me to go and tell her grandmother, "Now," they persisted.

I knew her mother had died, and I felt sympathy for her. The children carried on about how I shouldn't continue to ignore what had occurred, and then they repeated, "It is the right thing to do, Tanty." Many of the children who played regularly at my house gave me that name which means "Auntie".

They wore me down. The decision to walk over and talk to Agnes turned out to be one of the worst decisions that I ever made in the village and continues to torment me.

The approachable young father of Agnes was sitting outside his home on a wooden chair in his large clean courtyard, probably swept by Agnes, where he warmly greeted me with outstretched arms.

27

I asked to see his daughter, but he insisted that I tell him first what it was concerning. I reluctantly told him about the eggs, and I explained that I thought it was important that I should have a little talk with her and that it wasn't a big deal.

"Pas de grande chose," I kept repeating.

Her father calmly called out her name. Agnes sheepishly appeared before him, and then he violently grabbed the young, frightened girl by her thin little arm and began brutally beating her with a large stick he conveniently kept nearby. Both Agnes and I were screaming and crying, and I begged him to stop. Then her aunt jumped in and inflicted a twisting pinch. I ultimately pulled her away from them. At that moment, we were deluged in torrential rain. It was like a living hell with little Agnes screaming in pain. The sky had turned black. I was overcome with regret and remorse and slowly walked back home sobbing from the horror of it all through the mud, rain and under the mighty thunderclouds.

I noticed the town madman barefoot and in rags on my left along the way tied up to a tree howling in the mud to whoever would listen. It was a disturbing realization of how much worse he had it in so many ways, more than any of us.

The deafening rain continued to punish me as I shut my front door and decided that I never wanted to see anyone in the village ever again.

The brutal incident instigated the beginning of my overly optimistic crusade to end corporal punishment in the village. As it happened, I was not very effective. I began to learn which kids were abused near me, and whenever I heard the then familiar heartbreaking sound of a beating, I dropped everything and ran over to interrupt.

My two questions to a stunned father were always the same, "Were you ever beaten by your parents?" The answer was always, "Oui."

Then I would ask, "Did you ever learn a lesson from being beaten?" The second answer was always "Non."

"Find another way to teach a lesson!" I begged him.

It was said during Peace Corps training, "You never really know what effect you have on people," so I continued to ask the same questions and to interfere whenever possible even though I knew it was likely that I was not changing their behavior. Child abuse is a highly detrimental and pervasive issue within society and I would persist in my meager efforts to wipe it out.

The word began to spread around the village, "Learn English and play chez Mme Patricia outside her front door on the covered terrace."

Eager young children assembled almost every evening and, on the weekend to hang out, sing songs, or make bubbles. Their favorite book was "The Three Bears" and they would repeat word for word the sentences in the book because they heard it so many times. They also enjoyed learning the song "My Bonnie Lies Over the Ocean" or when I brought out the detergent or a bar of soap while teaching about the importance of hand washing for disease prevention. When my sister Janet sent me a bottle of strawberry scented liquid soap, there was a fight over who could wash their hands first, and there was no problem with the 45 second scrub rule.

"Kill the microbes!" we repeated while making bubbles from the soap.

My sister Liz sent a giant box of paper, colored paper, crayons, markers, pens and pencils and little scissors. If I wasn't in the mood to play, I always had the back-up plan, "It's art day".

The children also liked to see my photo albums, especially the one with my nephew Mickey and his beautiful bride, Mary, at their fairytale wedding that my sister Nancy had sent me, since I had missed the big event while in Africa. There was also the possibility that I would pass out a "bisquit" or a "bon bon" for a treat that many of the parents could not afford to offer them.

29

My #1 house rule was clear, "I almost always welcome you between 8 AM and 8 PM. Otherwise, the door is closed." I acted surprised in the mornings whenever I opened the front door to see who was waiting outside to greet me with a "Bonjour, Madame Patricia." It was usually cute little four-year-old Willie and his friends, Dibi, Blanche, and Alain, who, upon seeing me, would scream with delight and then hightail out of there as fast as they could run.

Figure 5 My little friends Dibi, Blanche, Willie, Alain

Figure 6 Hanging out in the village

Figure 7 The Chief of Braffouéby, Abo

Mr. Postman

There was one man in Sikensi, the largest town nearby, who enraged me, the Postmaster. He was very tall with a strong presence like my father's but lacked even a modicum of humor, kindness, or gentility. He alone worked at the post office and called me "Pot See', most likely because many of my letters were addressed to "Patsy", but most knew me as Patricia which I preferred, and sounds melodic in French. During workdays, I would check for mail before the two-hour mid-day closing break. It was impossible to sweet talk this man, as I found out the hard way. He was a "man's man." I had to remain polite to him regardless of the circumstances as he had the power and authority to hand me my packages and letters. Moreover, the ever-present long queue was dreaded, where other men often think nothing of cutting in line ahead of me. I was a mere woman. The postman would look past me and blatantly take care of the men around me, despite the rules of being "in line". His rudeness always set me off for a fight, so by the time he finally did acknowledge me, I was in a foul mood. I believed he broke into my boxes, or he was holding on to my letters, just to be a jerk.

There are numerous stories of people who mailed me things that I never received. My brother, Felix, and his wife, Linda, sent me a whole miniature Christmas tree with tiny ornaments to decorate that I would have loved. The broken box arrived long after the holiday with only a mangled tree with one bulb. Whenever the Postmaster handed me a box that was obviously opened by him, he would look at me straight-faced and say, "La douane." He blamed it on customs. I never believed him. My older sister Nancy sent me my mother's sweater that never arrived. My friend Sara wanted to replace the sandals that had disappeared outside my door. The first box of new Merrill sandals never arrived. I asked her to please send me one shoe at a time because if the shoes were together, there would be a greater possibility that I would never receive them, a hot tip I learned during training. Who would want to steal one shoe? The scheme worked, and I eventually received the pair. Carine, my good adult friend, called him *"sauvage,"* but anyone she didn't like was known as a savage.

Oscar

Oscar was a frequent visitor in the evenings. He was stricken with polio when he was only six years old, and was paralyzed except for the use of his hands. He was confined to a wheelchair and always dependent on someone assisting him. He was rejected by his father when he became handicapped, and his mother moved away when he was young, but his loving grandmother and beautiful aunts, Agate and the late Cecile cared for him, as well as many other generous people in the village.

Even though Oscar requires someone nearby to assist him with everything he does, he always managed to be wheeled over to my place to participate in evening activities. It was a welcome delight to see his big brown sparkling eyes absorbing every lesson. He told me once that there were people in the village who checked in on him often and made sure that he had enough food, or they would ask if he needed any help with something like going to the "toilette" (which meant the weeds) or to turn him over in his bed (which was a mat on the floor) in his small dark hut. He relied on others to push his wheelchair down the long hard, bumpy red clay road for over an hour to get to the high school in Sikensi and then back again in the evenings and wherever else he needed to go. Because there was a 2-1/2-hour school lunch break, Oscar stayed on campus during that time when teachers often found books for him to read while the others walked home. Sometimes he would be trapped at school in the late afternoon until someone would rescue him to push him home. Since it is rare to find books in the villages or in the schools, he profited from his lunch-break time because he was curious, possessed both high intelligence, and tenacity. He graduated number one in his class at the regional high school comprised of students from 15 different villages. He once wryly remarked, "What else did I have to do but study?"

There is a school for handicapped children in the next village, Bécedi, where Oscar excelled in primary school, and there, he was taken under the wing of the great Sister Catherine also from Bécedi, who furnished his wheelchairs and paid his school expenses. She was humble, gentle, and kind. Sister Catherine not only helped to support Oscar, but I later learned she was a key figure in contributing to the success of the future clinic in Braffouéby. Oscar demonstrated by his strong will and intellect that being "handicapped" is not a deterrent to success and showed me and the Ivorian world a new dimension of what being handicapped meant.

Oscar was a serious student and attended the university on a scholarship in the capital, where he studied mathematics and computer science. Unfortunately, the Ivoirian second civil war erupted in 2010, fought over a disputed political election that closed all the schools and the marketplaces. Because of the crisis, blockades were installed everywhere in and around Abidjan. The war took a heavy toll on the people, where about 3000 soldiers and many civilians were killed, and it was devastating to people already suffering from poverty. The war came to an end in April 2011 after enduring the arduous span of five months.

However, the lingering aftermath of the war persisted, leaving a lasting effect. After finishing two years, Oscar never returned to the university because somehow, the funds dried up.

Grade School

Why didn't I ever have a nun in my life like Oscar's Sr. Catherine, a nun who would be a mentor or a role model? No, I had the likes of the wretched Sr. Theolinda, who was a hanging dark cloud that impacted the future possibility of me ever having any relationship with a teacher. I feared the sight of her and figured all of the nuns were like her.

I was excused from class one day to go to the girl's room, and to my surprise, my best friend and only friend, Patty, from another class, was already there. We started jabbering away until suddenly we heard the rustling of rosary beads and the clomping of feet from the clunky black nun shoes she wore coming closer to us from down the hallway. We knew that we were both back in trouble because we were dallying. Impulsively, we hid in the last stall, locked the door, and stifled our giggles. Neither one of us thought it through about how obvious it appeared with the locked door and our four feet showing down below. We could hear her coming closer, and we anticipated the worst. She began banging on the door, screaming at us to open it up until we gathered up the courage to face the consequences. She grabbed me by my ear in her right hand and the collar of Patty's shirt in her other hand and marched us down the long hallway past all the open doored classrooms on the way to the principal's office.

During our long humiliating walk, she looked at me and kept repeating, "You dirty, dirty girl."

We arrived in the office of the most feared nun of all, the Principal, Sr. Salome. We were told to bend over the desk where she paddled our butts with what she called "the board of education." "Bam bam bam bam," echoed down the hallway along with my screams. "Dirty,

dirty girl!" echoed in my head. I used to think she was talking about the toilet being dirty until it was years later that I realized she thought we were having some kind of sordid sexual activity in that stall which was, at the time, the furthest thing from our naïve little minds.

If I couldn't remember the answer to a multiplication table, I was afraid Sr. Theolinda would grab me by the hair and pound my head on the desk, like she did to the boy sitting next to me until he came up with the correct response. The pimply purple pug-nosed nun with her tiny squinty eyes hiding behind her round wire glasses stood near my desk, always ready to say, "Wrong Nau," if I ever dared to answer a times table question incorrectly. I had a visceral fear of her and stayed home in bed, feigning an illness as much as I could get away with, all the while reading the 12 volumes of the Storybook Trails, the Mrs. Piggle Wiggles tales, and every biography I could get my hands on from the library. I had a bedside radio and listened to Patsy Cline and Elvis endlessly and the old 40's and 50's music that my parents played. I was hiding out from the nuns, and my classmates, whom I believed never liked me, except for Patty.

In grade school, I liked to pretend I was invisible because the kids called me "Coke Bottle Eyes" because of my thick glasses. I was funny looking with a chipped front tooth, a big gassy stomach, and straight fine hair that had a wild-looking wave on one side. I often found solace at home in a walk-in closet my mother gave me in the playroom with my own little table and chairs. My dolls and my husband John were my imaginary family, the Frugnuts. My dad was the doctor when one of "my girls", Susie or Janie, was sick. I loved that he played with me.

One day on the playground in 7th grade, I remember when a group of popular girls was standing in a circle, and someone opened it up to let me in. I blurted something out, and the girls turned to look at me and laughed. It wasn't in a mean way that would have made me want to disappear. It was a spontaneous laugh. I had unleashed something.

Laughter, I learned, was key to having friendships and being included, and naturally, made everything more fun.

I was usually compared to my older sister, who loved school and did well. In the first week of seventh grade, Sr. Fides looked at me with disdain, shook her head, and muttered, "You are nothing like your sister, Nancy." Already, I had another nun problem. The nun had a designated corner of the room she called "Patsy's playpen," where she ordered me to stay out of her sight. It was a known fact that she preferred the boys, especially the altar boys.

At the time Nancy was a cheerleader, and thankfully, her squad chose me during try-outs to be on their team that year. I didn't believe that I had the moves or skills, but I knew and liked Nancy's friends. I was told by Charlotte and a few others that the only reason I ever made cheerleading was because of my sister. "So, what? I was a cheer-leader!" I thought that, somehow, that was a redeeming achievement, and I had finally arrived.

My Family

Home was often loud, busy and chaotic, with all seven of us finding our way under my parent's guidance. In the background, there was usually the sound of music from show tunes or Frank Sinatra playing on the stereo. Mother played the piano or one of us was practicing over all of the noise, sometimes with a baby crying or somebody fighting or chasing someone to say, "I got you last". Most importantly through it all, Mother kept us on a tight, nutritious meal schedule, mainly because my younger brother, Felix, at 4 years old was diagnosed with childhood diabetes. It was the only time I saw my mother cry.

My parents did their best to ensure that we remained fully engaged in activities and exhausted by days end. They kept us busy by facilitating our music and dance lessons or my three brothers taking part in a sport. Although my favorite thing was when they had parties which gave me an opportunity to hang around their adult friends who I found to be fascinating. I first learned about France from their friend, Ray Schaub who sparked my desire to learn the language and to study there.

On one of my dad's birthdays, while we were all at school, mother invited a large group of her favorite female friends over for lunch. With his charm, wit and knack for making people laugh, dad was the guest of honor. By the time we all filtered in, after the school bus dropped us off, the husbands started to arrive and the party continued into the night with cocktails fueling their joviality. Another of my favorite things growing up was the solid connection between my parents. It was obvious to me that they truly loved each other.

Figure 8 My grown siblings, Nancy, Patsy, Nick, Janet, Felix, Peter and Elizabeth

Figure 9 The last Christmas with the whole family before my mother died.

37

Figure 10 My parents, Pat and Mike, in Kenya

I was grateful to learn how much of a difference mother and dad both had made in our friends' lives. They developed relationships with them and listened to their stories, gave advice, laughed, enjoyed, and included them. I loved that if I was playing with my friend Joanie, they would invite her to come along with us to the swimming pool or wherever. When my dad gave me some money, he was generous and would give me a little extra "to buy something for yourself and also for your friend." My friend Mag often says, "Your parents were the only ones I listened to and they were the only ones who could ever reign me in!"

Village Life

One early morning in the village, at barely the crack of day, I opened the front door and cried out for help, "Au secours, au secours!"

In the middle of the night when the entire village was asleep, I was startled and feared for my life when I woke up to thousands of giant-sized bugs attacking my tightly tucked-in mosquito net. While I cowered under the covers, all I could hear was the "clack clack clack" of the hard-shelled bugs with their intense buzzing sounds banging into each other, battering my net and the walls. I felt under my pillow for my trusty flashlight to be able to see what those monstrous flying fiends were up to, not knowing if they would ever stop, but realizing I could not escape until they did.

When I opened my eyes early in the morning after finally falling asleep and happy that I survived the horror show, there was a thick dark carpet of dead bug carcasses covering my floor in ten-inch heaps all over the room. I knew my flip-flops were buried somewhere underneath. I had no choice but to make it to the front door in my bare feet terrified from the crackling and squishing sounds from every step, while holding my breath to escape the horrifying scene and finally to arrive outside and find Odette. My dear neighbor responded swiftly to my rescue and swept them all away.

Odette assured me, shaking her head, that it would never happen again and left me with her comforting words "This is so rare, so rare to ever happen!" She was comforting, but I was doubtful.

A while later, my neighbor friends decided that the demonic attacking bugs were attracted by my flashlight. I was warned emphatically, "Do not read in bed with your flashlight on." In my humble opinion, the major factor was that the roof was not completely attached to the outside walls of the house, which left a five-inch opening all around the perimeter. It was made clear to me that it would not be fixed by the owners. The attack could indeed happen again, and I would continue to take my chances at night and escape into my books with my trusty flashlight propped on my shoulder.

Samuel, Odette's husband, was tall, thin, and handsome and would flash his toothy smile when he passed by my house, usually with some nonsensical quip about meeting with him and his drinking friends under the giant leafy Ficus tree. For most of the day, they pounded bangi wine or koutoukou, a dangerously strong distilled palm wine. He was full of happy talk, "Hey Patricia, what's the matter? Enjoy the day with us." He was easy to like with his infectious smile and his jolly good mood from the booze. I passed on his invitations.

As it was later sadly revealed, he was not that great of a guy. Odette now works in the fields in her cassava garden and laboriously makes *attiéké* under the hot sun to make a living, and her lazy husband, Samuel, who physically abused her, is dead from alcoholism. All of his happy talk and drink got the best of him. How blind was I to never know how much Odette suffered because of him, and like a saint, she never complained.

Agate was another caring neighbor who would come to sit with me in the evenings when the children weren't around. Sometimes we would sip a small glass of bangi wine she would supply. I listened intently as she spoke about her family and about the news of the village, including stories about those who had died and who had a baby.

People in the village normally depended on the charming young griot for their news. He walked around the village a couple times a week as the town crier and made general announcements in a vehement rhythmic cadence, but they were always in the Abidgi language, so I could not understand. It was a paid job, and he was a valuable part of the chief's men. He was eye candy, I confess, with enough charisma to be a movie star.

There didn't seem to be much interest in politics unless there was an election coming up when the discussions became intensely divided. But when it came to football, everyone agreed to cheer on team Eléphant Côte d'Ivoire! The people didn't get their news or sports from newspapers or television either since there were no newspapers sold or little money to buy them anyway. The word was that there were two small black and white TVs in the whole village. Boisterous crowds of boys and men spilled out of both houses to gather and watch the matches. One evening, I made my way to the front of the crowd at one of their houses to see the TV, but quickly turned around and left. I received non-verbal cues from the men craning their necks that I was blocking their view and basically, taking up space. The roar from the crowds echoed throughout the village like a small stadium whenever they were winning.

Agate's kind and gentle husband was a slight man, Philippe, who installed screens on my windows that were sorely needed because of the bugs, spiders, and mosquitos. The open area where the ceiling never met the walls required too many screens and would be too complex of a job, it was confirmed. He offered to hang curtains because my house was located mid-center in the village, and because he must have also seen the young boys peeking in at me. My curtain rods were ingeniously designed from bamboo poles made from trees that he brought in from the forest and fixed with nails to the walls in order to hang the new curtains. Philippe's shy little four-year-old son adored him and trailed close behind, never more than two feet apart. Together they went everywhere, which was endearing and unusual because it was the women who tended to the children, but this young child was lovingly attached to his dad.

Philippe looked pleased as he viewed his fine craftsmanship at the windows. The new curtains were made from *pagne* carefully stitched by one of Oscar's aunts, Celeste, a lovely talented seamstress. I was not aware at the time that there were so many different grades of *pagne* and that I chose the highest quality available. The women could immediately distinguish the difference, and in fact, one female guest in my house was aghast that I had curtains made from a grade of *pagne* that is used only for the finest clothing. It was much less expensive than any fabric like that I had ever seen in the States, and I loved the color and the pattern of navy and yellow.

"Patricia," she clucked, "non non non! Il ne faut pas faire comme ça," and so I was chastised for being wasteful by a teacher's wife, and at the same time was pointing to items in my house that she wanted me to leave to her. I just arrived, for godsake. I later regretted that I ever invited her into my house because she was always ready with a critical or unappreciated remark. She and her husband were not from the region and I rejoiced at the news that her husband was transferred to another school.

Phillipe's screens on my windows offered some protection, but one evening, something bit me at home. Odette and Agate thought it was a spider. My leg from the knee down was swollen to twice the size. It was red, throbbing, and intensely painful. The Peace Corps warned us not to partake in the traditional medications that they used, but I needed urgent care. Agate and Odette ordered a young child to summon the specialist skilled in their traditional medicine to come quickly to my house for a visit. The medicine woman arrived looking like she had been out working in the fields all day dressed in a worn-looking old faded *pagne* with an equally faded t-shirt and headwrap.

She was smiling and reassured me that she was there to help, "Patricia, calmez-vous. Je suis là."

I began feeling hot and woozy all over, along with excruciating pain. As soon as she arrived and assessed the situation, she sat me upright in my wooden chair and ordered another child to fetch some milk down the road in Sikensi. The woman left my place and returned with some herbs and then immersed my leg in a milk and herb concoction inside a plastic bucket. And she placed a black smooth rock on my leg. I was too far out of it to see how she formulated the remedy, and later, when I inquired, I was told that it was a secret of her trade. The cure started taking effect within a half hour. The village women were the ones not only giving life but saving lives too, and I was one of them that evening who was saved.

Many months later, I was bit again but I was already on my way to the infirmary anyway for my stomach. When the doctor treated my swollen foot, as I live and breathe, she placed a black smooth rock on it too, besides whatever else she did.

My Best Friend

Carine introduced herself to me early on during my stay in Braffouéby, impressing me with her accomplishments. She was shunned by most of the other people around, I noticed, and she didn't care much for them either. I thought that maybe she wasn't liked because of her success. Carine had a business sense and was ambitious. She owned and managed two restaurants, had a car, wore pants most of the time, instead of the traditional *pagne*, and had even traveled to Germany. I was surprised to learn that she was married twice and had children because she didn't seem to be much of a nurturer. She had a big presence and laughed easily, spoke loudly, and was opinionated and controlling, but I was fascinated by her strong personality.

I did not like the way she treated the staff at her restaurant, who would often cower when she was near. Carine would bark commands or criticisms at them and diminish their spirit by calling them "stupide" or "sauvage" or would shake her head disapprovingly, making loud clicking noises.

I asked her once, "Why are you treating your staff like that?"

She answered me with, "That is the only way these young girls will learn anything, the savages."

I defended the girls and disagreed with her many times, but it went to deaf ears. The truth was that the girls stayed to work for her because they needed the money, and there were few other options available to them.

When Carine would drive over to pick me up to take me to her open-air restaurant in Sikensi, she was always annoyed at the children playing around my house and often asked me why I tolerated them. When we arrived at her maquis named Kuwait, she made it clear to me saying that she "only wanted rich people to eat there."

Admittedly, it was always a treat to go anywhere in a car and her food was carefully prepared and delicious. The added bonus was that she served beer and wine. Sometimes she would make something German with potatoes, a rarity in the Ivory Coast. She was an anomaly, and I trusted her. When Carine invited me to her home and maquis, she often introduced me to many accomplished and interesting people whom I thoroughly enjoyed at lunches that would last for hours.

She told me that as a child, she and all nine of her siblings were often forced to stay home from school in Braffouéby and work in the fields to help support the family. Her enormous family of distinguished people was unusual in that most were well-educated and had professions. One of Carine's elder sisters always had a kind, beaming smile ready to flash whenever I saw her, a respected wise woman who raised many of her grandchildren while working on endless committees to help raise the standards of the village. I met another of her bright and successful sisters who lived in London, and I always enjoyed her wit and intelligence. Her brother was an affable English teacher at the high school. I would often find him in his courtyard surrounded by his friends and former students, discussing the world at large. Another quirky character was the lovable drunk, usually seen making small talk and cracking up about some kind of nonsense while bumbling around the village. Another worked at the port, drove a Mercedes, and always had different girlfriends in his large house furnished with a couch and chairs and framed cardboard pictures on the walls hung up close to the ceiling. Most of his neighbors did not own furnishings other than wooden chairs or benches to move around for outdoor gatherings. Carine was my trusted friend. I believed that underneath her crusty exterior was a kind and generous woman. Occasionally, she would let down her mean girl role to reveal her playful sense of humor and kind heart. I found the women to be the most fascinating.

The Women

Sometimes I enjoyed wandering around the village to see what kind of adventure I would find during my favorite part of the day after work before the blazing sun was about to set every day around 6 PM. There were always children to accompany me chatting and singing non-stop by my side, leading the way. The village at that time of day is engulfed in a magical golden light with larger-than-life shadows that overtake the open spaces on the hard-packed red Earth. There is a burst of energy in the air before nightfall while the older kids are playing their last game of football before heading home, and the babies and young children are getting soaped and scrubbed in a plastic tub by their mamas in front of their homes. There were no streetlights at the time,

44

and most people would soon be lighting their kerosine lamps, but not until it was pitch black outside so as not to waste any fuel.

One evening before dark, I met an old woman with weathered skin seated on her stoop. When I greeted her, she smiled widely showing her brown broken and missing teeth. I felt that I shouldn't hurry away, so I stopped to spend a moment with her. It made me think of John Prine's song "Say Hello in There, Hello," which he sang so poignantly about an older person who might be lonesome. She reached out to touch my hand while she spoke to me in a weak voice, and I could feel her strength through her penetrating yet cloudy gaze. I couldn't understand her message in Abidgi. It didn't seem to matter. She didn't know much French because she probably never went to school, so we never had a real conversation, but we understood each other. Her face and body were tired and worn from the many years of hard work under the brutal sun. She undoubtedly worked in the fields like most women without animals or machines to help her on the family's land located miles away. She probably packed a machete and some food wrapped in an old *pagne* to carry for the long hike. And most likely, her baby was tied to her back wrapped in another *pagne* as she set off to work at daybreak down the long rural dirt road. I knew she fetched water from the well as part of her daily chores and balanced the heavy vat on her head, which damaged her young neck as a girl. She gathered wood from the forest also balanced on her head to carry the unruly-looking load home to build the daily fires to prepare the family meals, which resulted in the smoke badly damaging her lungs and eyes. And she had worms from the water, like most people, which weakened her immune system making her more prone to illnesses. She could have been injured during childbirth at an age much too young, and the odds are that she did not have a devoted husband. Her story was like many women who lived in the village and who continue to inspire me with their dignity, courage, and joy.

One morning during training in Alepé there was a neighbor woman preparing to leave for her day in the fields to tend the crop, but first, she performed an enema of a burning herbal concoction on her one-year-old baby to induce an immediate bowel movement. The mother wouldn't have to attend to the child later while she was working or walking the three to nine miles with the baby attached to her back. The practice is frowned upon now as the women have learned that the practice resulted in the children having lower GI issues where the bowels would no longer function. I saw some of the toddlers screaming like holy hell and running away when they could.

Most families own a patch of land or at least have use of someone else's terrain. The women prepare food and perform the daily household chores and work in the fields with the cassava and maybe another vegetable. However, the men work in the cocoa, palm, banana, or rubber tree plantations which do not require as much labor. The everyday food, especially *manioc* (cassava) is usually harvested after twelve months and cultivated by the women. The plant is especially suited for the West African climate since it is pest resistant and can survive in a drought. The tuberous nutty-flavored fibrous root serves as the main food source and contains carbohydrates and some vitamin C.

Figure 11 Young girl carrying home the wood

Figure 12 The 6 PM shadows in the village

At The Market

Every Sunday, the local women and young girls, still dressed up in their best *pagne* dresses from church, parade around to meet their friends and buy what they need at the market when prices and selections are better and most of all, it was the time and place to see and be seen.

"Who wants to walk with me to Sikensi?" I called out one Sunday after church to any child listening.

"I do, I do". Tanty, please may I carry your backpack. Mai carried it last time."

My quickly assembled young crew took off with me down the road, still bickering over who would have the grand honor of carrying my backpack. The plus side was that they always managed to make the walk more entertaining. I was fully aware that there was an underlying hope that I would buy them something, anything, from a pair of rubber flip-flops to a lollipop.

It was shocking to see a young girl who had to weigh under 100 lbs hurl a huge sack of oranges to balance on her head that I myself tried to lift but struggled. They all giggled when they saw my feeble attempts at weight lifting and balancing.

The market is full of eye-opening sights. We arrived to see the town bustling as usual with vendors set up from many Arab countries, who came in from the north of Cote d'Ivoire and from all over Africa to sell their meats and create displays of bright, colorful vegetables and fruits and everything else a villager would want or need on market day. The children trailed behind me as I navigated the crowded narrow aisles overflowing with household goods and stacks of produce until I came upon my favorite stall.

There were three charming young women working under the main canopy who were always having a great time while selling peanut butter from a giant metal vat. I would look inside of it with interest because there are few things in the world that I enjoy more than peanut butter and people having a great time. There, I would see, never fail, dead flies burrowed in and around the top of the container and a couple of assorted spoons peeking out of the brown gooey paste that they never bothered to rescue. As much as I loved peanut butter, I found the flies rather unappetizing. I used to tell them to please keep the lid on because of the "microbes" from the flies. I didn't ever mention the spoon issue. It became a little game with them that every time they would see me coming, they would quickly cover up the bowl, and then we would all break into laughter. They didn't want to hear the microbe story again and they were not going to keep a cover on the top, no matter what. That day was no different and so the children heard the microbe story again with their glazed-over eyes until I got their attention by landing on a story about the microbes being tiny little monsters ready to eat them.

Before the walk down the bumpy road to Sikensi, I asked a group of my favorite neighbor women, "May I bring some beans back for you to try because they are delicious and packed with protein?"

They were delighted at the offer and promptly answered, "Oui, oui bien sûr."

Dried beans are not a usual part of their diet, but I urged the women to prepare them because of their nutritional value and I believed them to be affordable.

The children lead the way on the hunt for the beans at the Sunday market in Sikensi. I found it amusing that people refer to the rambunctious children who tag along with me as "petit bandits." The little bandits and I filled an extra-large-sized bag with a good sampling of every bean that they had. It seemed crazy to waste so many individual plastic bags, thinking of how the plastic bags would be carelessly discarded, so I naively decided to mix all the beans together. I obviously was not a fan of dried beans myself because I could not digest them and did not prepare them, but I knew they were nutritious. When I returned with the giant jumbled-up medley of beans, the women looked at me with gaping mouths expressing disbelief shaking their heads and clicking their tongues.

"Merci, Patricia pour le cadeau," but they couldn't spread their gift out on the ground fast enough to sort each one out into piles and get me out of the way. Everyone pitched in for the task. For some odd reason, they did not want me to help!

"Non, Merci beaucoup. Asseyez-vous!" They echoed. I was ordered to sit across from them and watch them as they diligently sorted each bean into its designated pile. After they completed the task, I walked back home feeling like a complete fool.

At that time, I didn't fully understand the consequences of children suffering from anemia because of their iron-deficient diet, but I did notice that many children were malnourished by their distended stomachs, thin little bodies, and some with obvious stunted growth.

I witnessed suffering and dying from the global health problem, malaria, combined with anemia. In severe cases, the malaria parasites can enter red blood cells, which rupture and cause anemia, often associated with neuro developmental delay in young children, or stillborn babies, or the death of the infected pregnant mother.

We are grateful to Vitamin Angels, who have, over the years, donated prenatal vitamins and vitamins for babies and children under 12 years to help prevent anemia. One day I am hopeful that there will be a vaccine for malaria which is in the final stages of development. Can you hear me, Bill and Melinda Gates Foundation, WHO and the World Bank?

Many years later, during a visit to the health clinic we built with the foundation donated by the Ministry of Health in Braffouéby, a young father arrived out of breath carrying his one-year-old anemic baby in a coma. He held the child close to his chest after walking with him for over two hours. He was frightened but determined and desperate to help save his life. I saw the baby's eyes flickering open and shut, and his ashen-colored body that was limp and not responding. The doctor provided intravenous antibiotics for him, which I thought was miraculous because after an hour, he came out of the coma, but he was still very weak and anemic. He probably should have had oxygen, which is almost impossible to obtain for rural health clinics because I was told by the Ministry of Health that oxygen is simply not available.

Many times, I have promoted a varied nourishing diet with fruit, vegetables, legumes, and peanuts, but people want to eat what their mothers served them. In reality, it always comes down to what one can afford to eat, where most are living in different degrees of poverty. In any case, the women did not want advice from me on what to eat or how to prepare their food.

"Madame, Madame Patricia, look, look what we have!"

I was sitting outside on my steps, still feeling stupid about the bean fiasco, when a couple of young boys came frantically running up to me. Their fists were full of torn-out paper ads for running shoes. They had found a catalog filled with items they had never seen, and that were not available to them in Sikensi or otherwise. One by one, they described in detail exactly what size shoe they wanted and the color and then asked if I would go to America as soon as possible and send them that specific pair of shoes. I thought about how every little boy has his idea of how a shoe should look and how much they dream about having the pair that they want. My own sons, who both loved shoes, were no different, except that I was usually able to fulfill most of their shoe dreams.

Figure 13 the path to Braffouéby

Figure 14 Outdoor kitchen

Figure 15 Making attiéké

Down Life's Path

I thought about Mike and Matt often and daydreamed about what they were up to while I was in Africa. Terry and I had two precious sons during our twelve years of marriage. The boys always have my heart. It took everything that I had to keep them challenged and happy. They were a joy, smart and creatively mischievous. I had married my high school sweetheart, and when they were 5 and 10 years old, after 12 years of marriage, I divorced the "couch potato," as he was nicknamed. I subsequently went through all of the emotional, practical and financial challenges that go along with divorce.

I was peeking around the corner of the "recreation room" during my older sister Nancy's freshman year high school party, and I got caught. I was a lowly eighth grader who was checking out my big sister's classmates and my eyes landed on one especially tall and handsome football player, Terry. I was mortified when he saw me watching him. With my heart racing, I ran up to my room, not having the courage to have a conversation. He asked my sister that night to be "fixed up with me" when I became a freshman. And then it all began.

Our first date was on a hayride when we drank bourbon out of a bottle, and I lost a contact lens on the hay wagon. Terry almost immediately gave me his high school ring, which meant I was taken. Many times, over the years, I would break up with him because I felt stifled and not understood, but he was handsome, popular and the quarterback which was important in my adolescent mind. I would always go back to him because he never went away.

My dad drove my sister and I to high school in the mornings. We were always racing across the numerous sets of train tracks in NW Indiana before another train would stop us and make us late. He would often pick up our friends, Bobbi and Mary, along the route in need of a ride. It was usually a pleasant time unless my older sister was fighting with dad for more freedom which also, by the way, benefitted me and my social schedule. Dad had three cardinal rules. In his loud booming voice, he would repeat, "Beach parties OUT, carnivals OUT, drive-in movies OUT." How could the three most fun things to do with my friends in high school be OUT?

When Terry came calling at my house the first time during my freshman year and every time after, he said that he just put his hand up to the door, and it shook by itself. "I didn't even have to knock," he said half in jest. Dad, whose commanding presence would elicit fear in young men, made it difficult for my sisters and me to date. He insisted on meeting the friend first, before I could have permission to go out with him.

The University of Arizona was the "#1 party school" in 1964, according to Playboy magazine when I enrolled. I was somewhat embarrassed by its reputation but thrilled at the opportunity. I would be in the warm sunshine every day and be a part of a large college campus made up of students from all over the world. It sounded so very exciting after living in northwest Indiana, with steel mills and manufacturing and then move into a cowboy town filled with Saguaro cactus in the desert.

When my parents said good-bye to me in front of my college dorm, my mother soberly stated, "Patsy, you will have your baby blues wide opened." My dad left a note in my mailbox with his drawing of an umbilical cord with some scissors and the quote, "snip."

After eagerly looking forward to attending my first fraternity party, I was sexually molested during the event. I completely misread the predator's fun-loving, energetic vibe. He was tall and had that clean-cut winning kind of east coast preppy look. We strayed from the main room of the party carrying our heavily spiked punch concoctions over to a side room with a lot of windows and a long couch where we sat down together, all cozy, I thought. I saw his eyes flash me a disturbing look while, at the same time, he aggressively pounced his heavy body on top of me while grabbing me everywhere he shouldn't, under my skirt and down my blouse at my breasts. There was no fun-loving banter, or locked loving gaze, no sweet kiss, and no warning. I finally managed to escape from beneath him. Hurt and horrified by his assault, I ran all the way back to my dorm, shaking with fear and revulsion. I felt violated and dirty but never told anyone because fraternity parties were supposed to be fun, and I was afraid to call attention to myself that way. What was I doing to bring that on? I hid in my room while everyone was out that night and cried myself to sleep. I hadn't made any close friends yet, so I buried what happened to me deep down inside forever. I felt guilty and ashamed.

The next day I was destroyed and humiliated once again when a girl who was at the same party casually informed me that he had told everyone that I had sex with him.

I can still hear her spitting out the words, "Way to go, Patsy... easy lay... at the first party."

"Great," I thought, "I am now... officially...a slut."

I joined a sorority and was named during the Delta Gamma pinning ceremony "Worst Pledge" and also was called a "Late Bloomer" because I was not much of a contribution to the stellar reputation of the house in that, I was not a homecoming queen or queen of anything, for that matter. I hid out in the dorm my freshman year as much as I could. During that year especially, I was self-conscious about meeting new people and gravitated towards my friends in the dorm where I lived. After the demeaning titles I was given, I became even more apprehensive, anxious, and self-conscious. The sum of it all ruined almost every encounter that I had with men that I met. I didn't trust anyone, and only went out with people I knew and preferred to be in groups. During my sophomore year, we were required to move into the sorority house and I slowly came to appreciate my lively and accomplished new group of friends.

The University of Pennsylvania had a junior year study abroad program where I enrolled and was eager to begin a new chapter. Five students boarded the SS United States Ocean Liner in New York City's port to spend nine months at the picturesque University of Grenoble situated in the French Alps, the year before the 1968 Olympic games there.

I met a kindred spirit on campus, Beth, who was very keen on adventures. Her Hollywood experiences were different from my own growing up in the Midwest. She smoked pot and had sex at age 13 and had traveled all over Europe, and also was intent on continuing her travels. Beth found her housing with a fancy banking family in a stately mansion in town, and I lived with a Moroccan family outside the city in a nondescript suburb filled with apartments built for immigrants, which was not easy to find.

After checking in to the university, I hauled my giant suitcase from place to place, scratching off addresses from a list that the registrar had posted on a bulletin board because there was an "unanticipated housing shortage." Nobody had phones, of course, and wheels on suitcases hadn't been invented yet. I took some taxis and became frustrated when the drivers could not understand me. It was getting dark, and a room located outside of Grenoble was the last place on the list. There was a bus to the concrete jungle they called Fontaine, where I found my new home amid a sprawling compound of bland blonde brick low-rise apartment buildings with no landscaping. I was exhausted to at last find a room and meet Mme. Ortega outside the door. Her big dark eyes, shiny black hair, and radiant smile warmly greeted me. She carried my suitcase up the cement stairs to their apartment on the second floor. My cramped room with a double bed and light-colored armoire in front of it hardly had enough space to walk around it. I could not have been happier.

Madame's short, thick-bodied husband with black curly hair and dark whiskered face was often off working on the railroad. When he was home, he would occasionally knock on my door at night. His deep-set black eyes darted from side to side when he offered me a glass of his home-distilled liquor that tasted like fuel. He was kind and gentle, with a burly chuckle that made me laugh. I looked forward to an invitation from Madame to their Sunday family dinner to devour the different cumin and turmeric-flavored tasty stews of couscous with lamb or chicken, but I always felt like I was eating food that they could barely afford because of the small portions. Often ravenous, I was surviving on cafeteria food at school where tripe was the bargain dish.

Years later, I learned that tripe was stomach linings from farm animals and never had it again.

I bought a box of couscous at the market to make at home in America. I never figured out how to make it because the directions said to place it in a coucousière which stumped me. When I moved to Chicago from Munster, I still guarded the box of couscous as a cherished souvenir, serving as a gentle reminder of the warm-hearted family I had in Fontaine.

Madame tended to the two primary school-aged children while Monsieur was working on the trains. Catherine, their youngest, was obsessed with Cher and only wanted to talk about her and Sonny as if I knew the famous singing duo from the States, but chatting with her about Sonny and Cher gave me an opportunity to practice my elementary-level French language skills.

There was a ritual in their home which was about saving money and keeping the apartment clean. When a family member entered the house, she explained, "You take off your shoes by the door and then place your feet on your own cut-out felt footprints and then glide to wherever you are going in the apartment," and then she showed me how it was done. If I ever lifted my foot, I would lose my felt foot cutout, which was not good. It was a learned skill probably from Morocco that I never completely mastered because of my lack of coordination, nor did I learn the French word for their curious practice. It cost less money to buy a piece of felt rather than a pair of house shoes, I figured. They kept most of the lights off, and they often reminded me when bathing to only run the water to get wet, turn it off to soap up, and then rinse off. The bucket baths and mindful use of electricity many years later in the African village were not a problem because of my already-learned respect for water and electricity.

Beth, my new friend in Grenoble, was a male magnet. With Beth around, there were men. Since our classes were so large, there were no roll calls or assigned seats, so we took the liberty of attending school or not. I loved our day trips on the train to Geneva, Switzerland to eat chocolate and cheese fondue. We usually hitchhiked towards Provence or the Cote d'Azur but took a train whenever we were flush with money when traveling to Spain, and all over Italy at every chance we could. When faced with a situation with men, which often began as fun and amusing, I soon felt that sickening fear from the assault my freshman year and became highly skilled in what is known as the "French exit."

Our most adventurous trip was when we took a cruise on a Greek ship to Athens and the Greek islands, and attended mass on Christmas Eve in Bethlehem right before the war in 1967. One afternoon during our trip, we narrowly escaped a Bedouin tribe deep in the desert outside of Tel Aviv who began chasing us in their long, flowing black robes with long sticks while throwing stones at us after we attempted to visit their camp. The cab driver warned us, but we were too stubborn to listen. Thank the Lord, the cabbie waited for us while we ventured out. I was later informed that the nomadic people do not tolerate outsiders, which was clear.

While hitchhiking one long weekend on our way to Mallorca, the driver suddenly turned off the main road down a side road into a wooded area. We both went on high alert and asked our driver in broken Spanish where he was headed, and we pleaded with him to turn around, but he ignored us. Beth, savvy as ever, signaled for me to follow her lead. She made the sign of the cross multiple times, back- ward, I noticed, and I followed suit the Catholic way and added some "Santa Marias" for extra gravitas. She was aware that many Spanish people have deep religious roots and deduced that praying would thwart him. It worked. He apologized, and in the end, the driver took us all the way to our destination. I said some real "Santa Marias" afterward, grateful to emerge unscathed.

Grenoble and the Alps in 1967 were bustling with preparations for the 1968 Olympics games to be held there. The town itself was trans- formed before our eyes, with the Swiss-feeling downtown was being closed off like a mall, most roads were under construction, and new modern buildings were popping up everywhere.

I was a beginner on the slopes where we rented the extra-long, old-styled skis. The drill was that one extends a right arm reaching towards the ceiling, and then you flap your hand over the top of the ski to determine the height of the skis that you rent, which was the usual manner of measuring. I couldn't afford lessons and learned the old-fashioned way, by picking up random helpful advice along the way. I broke my knee on the icy last run of our last day at Les Deux Alps near Grenoble at the end of the season and was transported on a stretcher to the infirmary. In those days nobody was able to fix that particular bone so I stayed on the bottom of a bunk bed alone and in pain for weeks, miserable without so much as an aspirin and bored out of my mind. When I was strong enough to use crutches, I found transport back to my own room in Fontaine. It took a calamity to keep me down, where I could only speak French and no English. My language skills noticeably improved.

The two semesters in France were ending in May, and it was nearing the end of April. I had no intention of spending the summer with my family in Indiana or seeing my old boyfriend. I was yearning for a new language and a new country, and many more adventures.

I began scheming. I needed a plan on how to extract permission from my parents to stay in Europe and, most importantly, to receive a check that would make it all possible. I settled on the idea of writing them and exclaiming how I found an excellent school in Germany where my grandfather was born. Beth described a place that she knew, and I, in turn, relayed that same information to my parents, stressing how important it was for me to better understand my heritage. How could they say no to a story if I brought up my grandfather?

The truth was that I didn't know where I wanted to go. After writing the letter, I heard about a School for Foreigners located in Perugia, Italy, but I had no information about it. The fact that it was in Italy was enough for me, and that someone knew someone who had visited there. The letter and check came during my last week of school in Grenoble. Elated, I packed my bags, bid adieux to my friends and the wonderful Ortega family, and traveled to sunny Perugia, Italy, for the summer!

It was loud and chaotic, just like home, as soon as I crossed the border from France into Italy. What a relief to find the school so accommodating after living through the Grenoble "no housing available" experience. Fortunately, they recommended a great little place to rent nearby down a very narrow winding street in the oldest section of town.

I walked up to the top floor of the ancient building on a corner of a tiny piazza, where I was greeted by Senora Bernini in a faded pastel flowered house dress and thin glasses she wore low on her nose. Standing about 4-1/2' tall, she wore her black and grey streaked hair tied in a bun. Since I had no English-speaking friends, I picked up the language easier than French, thanks to the kind tutelage from the Signora.

My dear old upstairs landlady often showed me off during the day to her customers who came by to have their fortunes told by reading their palms. When she read my palm, she said that I had a very short lifeline. She was quite troubled by her discovery, but she assured me that I had the power to change it. She sometimes knocked on my door for a visit to play "cos'è questo," aka "name this object." The Signora enriched my study sessions, and she took great pride in my progress. I looked forward to her visits and the variety of characters she brought over to meet me.

After class during the sunny afternoons, I would study my vocabulary and irregular verbs, usually dressed in my snakeskin bra and black panties with my workbook on my lap perched on the windowsill of my room. I thought my attire could pass for a swimsuit, and having a year-round tan was an important Arizona learned lesson and part of the culture there. And I loved the sun. Noticing men gathered from time to time on the street below, I occasionally, would flash a smile at them. One late afternoon I was disturbed by a loud pounding on my door, nothing like the gentle knock I was used to hearing. I threw a dress on and opened the door to see the Polizia standing next to the Signora. I understood that I was to be arrested "for soliciting." The lovely Signora wearing her same faded pastel flowered house dress strongly defended my character. She explained to them how she often visited me during the day and that I was like a daughter to her. The charges against me were dropped. I continued to bask in the sunshine at my window, but I promised her that I would study there only when I was fully clothed.

At 5 PM, it seemed that everyone in town went outside to "fare una passeggiata," which is the time when the townspeople walk around to meet friends and neighbors and have a caffè or an aperitivo. One evening, I sat at a café table near the same handsome man that I had eyed on an earlier occasion. After he moved his chair over a little closer to mine, he invited me to a party. We drove in his Ferrari outside of town to a castello high on a hilltop because I could not say no. I knew I was putting myself in a precarious position, but he seemed to be the man of my dreams. The party was magnifico with fine wine, loud music, and happy people's voices filling the air, but later that night, I knew from the way he was touching me and his murmurings in my ear that I had to find an exit strategy without the dreamy, handsome man or the Ferrari. He was giving me uncomfortable vibes, and he was not listening to my repeated requests to slow down.

"Lentamente," I repeated. My language skills were not that great.

Using the "looking for the bagno" excuse, I then asked anyone I saw near the cars if I could have a ride back to Perugia. The escape game was my only solution.

I immersed myself in the Italian culture. I took short train trips to Assisi, Siena, Firenze, and Roma, visited the museums and churches, and tasted every flavor of ice cream and pastry and the local wines, beer, and coffee. The restaurants were beyond my budget. My modus operandi would be to visit the town's postcard display and decide what I wanted to see, and then ask for directions. I was anxious to write my mother and dad to thank them for giving me this splendid opportunity.

I wrote them gushing on and on about my new daily Italian life, forgetting that I had asked permission to go to a school in Germany. I learned later from my mother that upon receipt of the letter, my father threw it up in the air and marched out of the house with his shaggy sheepdog, Mac. Dad wrote me a stern but funny letter reprimanding me, yet I knew that he was happy that I had found my perfect place. His letter made me laugh and love him more, if that was possible.

My next brilliant idea was to finish college and graduate from New York University instead of returning to Arizona. I didn't want to revisit the sorority life and be reminded of my fear of running into "the predator." In Europe, the conversations were about the war in Viet Nam and art, history, and philosophy. I could not go backward. This time after sending a letter to my parents with my latest plea, my mother responded almost immediately with her terse but wise command, "You will go back to the University of Arizona, you will graduate with your class, and you will find out that everyone has changed just like you have." And was my mother ever right!

When I first heard the song "Ask Alice" by Jefferson Airplane, I knew there was a whole new energy on campus. Nobody was wearing giant hair rollers in the sorority house, or sitting under the dryer, no more bras, girdles, or false eyelashes. I found my old friends who embraced me, peace-loving students on campus attending anti-war demonstrations and giving away flowers. What a difference a year had made.

I still did not know what I wanted to do after graduation since Liberal Arts left me with a wide array of choices. Soon after I returned, there were interviews taking place on campus, and my question was answered. With my two languages which were a prerequisite, I decided to continue my world exploration as a flight attendant for Pan American Airlines and hoped to be stationed in Hawaii with my college roommate. I was bubbling over with excitement when I told Terry and my family about my plans during Christmas break.

Alas, I became engaged over Spring Break to Terry, my first boyfriend. I was too young, a virgin, and naïve. It was a safe decision, I know now. I was away from him and my home for most of four years and I hardly knew him.

After returning to Indiana in late August after eleven months abroad, Terry took me out on glorious dates. He courted me in fine fashion. We visited a cool coffee house with beatnik vibes in Old Town and went to the fancy Trader Vic's to drink exotic Polynesian cocktails with floating gardenias at the Palmer House Hotel. We attended concerts and went horseback riding.

One night we saw Dr. Zhivago at the big movie house in the Loop, which was the most romantic movie I had ever seen, and then we fell asleep after "making out" in the front seat of the car in the parking lot. My dad was standing by the door waiting for us at home. Some things never changed.

Instead of meeting our friends in Chicago as Terry propositioned over Spring break, he proposed to me in his nothing special or romantic way.

"I will only ask you once," he repeated. It was a trap. I knew the big rush to get married was so that he wouldn't be sent to Vietnam, and possibly he feared that I would grow up, then leave him and fly away on a Pan American airplane. My self-doubt and insecurities played loudly in my head the remark from someone who said to me, "Nobody will ever love you as much as Terry."

We drove up to Detroit, where he knew of a jeweler from a school friend, where he unceremoniously bought me a diamond ring. With my left hand in my pocket, we surprised my parents after driving back to my house so that Terry could ask my father for my hand in marriage.

My mother was sitting in the living room, happy and surprised to see us, and with her signature giggle, she said, "You both look like the cat who swallowed a canary."

I discovered the thrill of being engaged. When my dad entered the room after giving me a big hug, he looked at Terry, greeted him, and asked if he would help fix the toilet. The thrill was killed.

I called Terry from Arizona after Spring vacation when I mustered up the nerve to ask him to delay the wedding, which was set for June. He agreed but only pushed it to July. I was sorely disappointed because I was hoping for another year, but I never asked for it. How could he know what I wanted if I never made it known? And why should he ever have to perform the impossible task of reading my mind? I was so immature. And besides, "Nobody would ever love me like him," I believed it.

My father tried to talk me out of getting married, which offended me, and at the same time, like a child, it made the idea more appealing. The invitations had already been sent out when dad approached me in June with an alternative. He said I could go anywhere in the world I wanted and that he would pay for it and "to hell if the invitations are already out." Dad gave me a way out, but by then, I was enjoying the spotlight and looking forward to the big party, my wedding.

I remember I suggested we blow through all the money people gave us for gifts on the big day and go somewhere and have fun. Terry had a very different set of ideas and made it clear that he was in charge, which was the first clue that I had lost my independence and that he had other priorities. He preferred to stay home and save money.

I was hurt when my new husband remarked that he didn't think I looked beautiful on the day of our wedding. "What a mean thing to say," I whimpered. He said, "You looked like you always do." I didn't wear a Pricilla of Boston silk organza wedding gown from Marshall Fields everyday. In all fairness, I had my hair done the morning of the wedding and hated it so much that I leaned over the bathtub and stuck my head under the faucet. It was the 60's when beauty shop hair from an Indiana salon did not fly with me or the current trends.

After our perfectly beautiful wedding in the parish church with my seven bridesmaids, followed by a large reception under a pink and white striped tent at an old English inn, and our fishing honeymoon on Jupiter Island, we moved to Cleveland. I had never fished before and haven't ever fished again but the island was beautiful. I was fortunate to find a job teaching high school French since I never took an education course during college. Teaching was never my plan. And fishing was not my dream honeymoon.

"And please, state to me your philosophy of education," the crotchety old nun asked me during my interview at the Catholic high school. Since I didn't have any kind of teacher training, I had no formulated response to the big question which is developed while following an education curriculum. A teaching certificate was not required at private school. I answered something flowery and absurd that must have registered with her, or she was so desperate for a French teacher that I was hired. I never fit in very well with the nun/teacher culture, which is why teaching at a Catholic school was an anathema to me.

"Mrs. Mertz, your skirt is too short."

"Mrs. Mertz, your homeroom is not decorated properly!"

"Mrs. Mertz, there is too much noise coming out of your classroom!"

Some days the principal would waddle over to sit in on one of my classes to give me some "constructive criticism." I was willing to be coached but not criticized. I would have gladly welcomed guidance, encouragement and strategies for improvement, but she was all about disapproval which was discouraging and demoralizing. I could often hear her footsteps and the familiar jingling of rosary beads nearing my door from down the hallway, getting closer, bringing that ominous black cloud that would loom over us all. Any good energy in the room was zapped.

I detested the crowded teacher's lounge where they all sat and gossiped about other students, the parents, and the siblings of the students. I could only imagine how my own crazy wild family must have been the target of teachers' attacks, not that many years ago in a school much like this one. There was a kindred spirit on the staff, a Spanish teacher from Argentina. Ramona liked to go outside to smoke and joke with me and eat the delicious bagels from the vending machine. She was a positive force full of great teaching ideas in a school full of negativity.

One afternoon, when the principal darkened my doorway without warning, she barked orders at me to follow her to the office. The familiar heart-pounding sensations from my memories in grade school washed over me as I sat down to face her.

She stood up, leaned over the desk towards me, and with her angry red face, in a menacing tone, she sputtered, "You...lied! You said you had graduated, and you... didn't!"

"What!!!"

I had no idea what she was talking about. She went on to explain that I needed two more credit hours on my transcript that had just arrived on her desk from Arizona. I wanted to disappear because this same scene was a real recurring nightmare coming true.

I could only say, "I didn't graduate?"

She handed me a copy of my transcript. In my most humble and sincere voice, I assured her that I would take a correspondence course for the 2 lacking credit hours, and I would fix the problem. I took a Spanish course soon after and received my degree in the mail as the class of 1969 instead of 1968.

Being born in 1946, when the first class of "baby boomers" hit the schools, the administrators were always scrambling to accommodate us. From the very beginning of my years in school, there were 60 children crammed in each first-grade classroom at St. Ann's grade school. During high school, we had freshman year in a grade school. Before our freshman year on campus, the university hastily built two new freshman dorms with four girls sleeping and studying in one small, crowded room. It included two bunk beds, one long "desk" table supplied with 4 chairs along one wall, and one giant closet between the two beds in the middle of the room with two doors on each side to cram your clothes on your side of the room. It should not have been a shock that the Baby Boomers were all coming!

My parents and fiancé came to Tucson to celebrate my college graduation, and we celebrated the grand occasion in high style. They had said that our diplomas would be mailed to us, but I was too busy as a new bride in a new city with a new career to be thinking about the whereabouts of my diploma.

At the beginning of the school year as a French teacher, I should have remembered every student's name and then had something worthwhile to say about each one on parent's day, which, in my opinion, came way too soon in the school calendar. I was sadly not prepared. Too many times, I drew a blank and gave generic descriptions like, "She really seems to enjoy learning" or "What a great student with so much potential." The experience was stressful, and I felt that I had let the parents and students down.

Terry and I were in a rhythm of going to work, cooking together, and fixing up our cozy, cute little coach house. We lived in an old, established residential neighborhood near his former university, where he became an Admissions Counselor, making him exempt from the draft, his goal. He liked his familiar college bars that we sometimes frequented, but I would often awkwardly run into some of my senior high school students drinking beer in the same places. Like reckless college youths, we drank too much and drowned out our feelings.

There was little interest in indulging myself with feelings of regret or disappointment. I was married and locked in.

There was one senior girl in my advanced class who was very bright with red curly hair and glasses, a National Merit Finalist with a gifted photographic mind. I had something extra for her to do or read during class most days because I felt intimidated by her and realized she needed more material. Even the brightest students were not able to keep up with her. She sat with both feet flat on the ground with her hands folded on top of her desk and stared straight at me, just the way the nuns always wanted me to do years ago. The rest of the class was probably used to her abilities because she was prepared, eager to learn, and very talented. I received a sweet note after she graduated, saying that I was her favorite teacher in the whole school, and she thanked me, which made my extra efforts feel worthwhile. I later discovered that she had become a nun.

We drove back to my house during Christmas break for our first holiday together. Under the tree, my father handed me a black leather-like fake book with the title written in gold on the spine, "My Travels to Hawaii by Patsy Nau." I was not amused by his teasing, but he knew that I had made a mistake by getting married, and he knew that by then, I had realized the same thing. I was already pretending to be happily married, and I avoided any negative thoughts, but dad could see through it. I was determined to make my marriage work after I squashed my dreams of more travel and becoming an international stewardess.

With a high fever and gasping for air a few days after Christmas, I was diagnosed with a severe case of pneumonia and was carried into the hospital to be placed on oxygen. A few days later, during a visit from Terry, I asked him to help me call the principal to let her know that I would be absent when school started.

The nun was her usual cruel self and responded with, "You couldn't have picked a better time, you know."

I wasn't sure how to respond to that type of remark, and I was too weak anyway, so I just handed the phone to Terry, who instantly hung it up.

The good news was that I stopped smoking cigarettes after experiencing a new respect for healthy lungs.

Terry made plans to start a janitorial service making floor wax back in Indiana. I was crushed. There was an opportunity in Arizona for him in a different business, but he wasn't interested. He made the decisions, I learned, and I was to follow. I cried and begged him not to go back to the "region," which was where we grew up.

To console me, Terry suggested we have a baby. I started thinking about the idea of having a child, and my spirits lifted. My parents offered us their summer log cabin high on a dune overlooking Lake Michigan to live in temporarily while Terry started his business.

Terry and I were harmonious in a way I had always imagined when I came home from the hospital with baby Michael right before Mother's Day in 1970. He was tuned in to the birth experience, his eyes were welled over with love for both of us, and he was present for me emotionally. We sat out in the garden near the ravine bursting with new springtime life, and I was happy and in love with him and our new little baby

"This is it!" I thought. I love my husband, and he loves me and our new baby boy.

We lived in my family's summer home in the dunes for almost three years, and I soon longed to have our own little place to live with our new family, free from the open-door policy set by my siblings and their friends. My plea was for a tiny house, a trailer... any place that could be ours with our things and our family. I smoked pot for the first time with friends one night when it smacked me in the face again that I should never have married. I gave up smoking pot until I was divorced.

I often thought about my lavish courtship and decided it was an attempt to capture me on false pretenses. He didn't really like to listen to classical guitar, go to plays, visit Chicago, or basically, go anywhere. When I eventually accused him of taking me for granted, he said, "Of course I do, you are my wife." When I would tell him how I was feeling, I had so much pent-up emotion built up inside of me that I came on too strong. He had taken some philosophy course in college about logic and said that I wasn't speaking logically, which gave him the license to walk away and shut the door in my face. Our relationship never grew, I felt like a prisoner, and we never resolved anything between us. One thing we were very good at which was showing the world how happy we were. Of course, I was the one pretending.

I continued over the years the same false narrative that I was in a happy marriage because failure was not a possibility, and divorce was out of the question. My brother called Terry "tick-tock" because he liked to be on the same schedule every day. Any variation was a struggle. But I made sure that we had a busy social life no matter what the struggle entailed. I immersed myself in playing tennis during the day which was good for my mental health, and we went to dinner with friends which included drinking a lot during the evenings of the weekends which made it all easier to endure.

In the West African village of Braffouéby, marriage, and divorce are very costly and considered to only be available to the most prosperous families. Many people with some money marry the traditional way, which includes a dowry of usually a bottle of African gin, and a cow, if possible, and several of the best quality colorful *pagnes* for the bride's family and some cookware, enough for their whole life, and of course, a big meal of foutou and *attieké* with sauces to feed the guests. The marriage ceremony is officiated by the chief and attended by the family and friends, who are usually dressed in matching *pagne* fabric made into boubous, caftans, and dresses created especially for the event. For divorce, the man just moves on and, in the best-case scenario, he helps support the children. The court costs and hiring a lawyer is simply, out of reach for most because of the fees.

The Abidgis of the Ivory Coast

All fifteen villages celebrate the Abidgi tribe on the first weekend of September for the "Festival des Ignames" or "Dipri." The descendants of the original five families of Braffouéby gather in the village and come in from far and wide for traditional rituals and feasting on *foutou* and *attiéké*.

Figure 16 Foutou

Figure 17 Attiéké

As dawn was breaking on the Saturday of my first festival of "Dipri", I woke up to a distant rumble from a crowd of people outside my bedroom window and then peeked through my curtain to see the throngs of people dressed in white flowing robes parading down the road. They were heading towards the path of abundant wild miniature pineapple and towering banana, avacado and mango trees with super-sized leaves to their secret ceremony at the spiritual hill, made of granite called *le Rocher*, the Rock. I was never clued in about many tribal details.

The children persuaded me to climb the towering granite rock with them one day before the feast. They giggled as they earnestly told me the story about the good and evil genies who lived there and ate the fruit, but the children had little interest in eating any of it themselves because they all agreed that fruit didn't fill their stomachs. "I am still hungry if I eat fruit" or Fruit is not satisfying" were common responses.

"How about eating it for their nutritional values" went to deaf ears or blank looks.

Since their traditions were oral, they told me the story of the "Rocher" that goes something like this: "There were three young girls who had gone in search of escargots in the forest. Two girls among them had collected a good quantity of red escargots, but the other one had only found one black escargot. When they returned to the village, the genie appeared to them. He asked the girls to give him the escargots. The two girls, who had a lot of them, refused to give him any. The genie made the same request to the girl who had only found one escargot. She agreed to give him her only escargot. After taking the escargot, the genie advised the one girl to immediately leave for the village without looking back. Once the girl left, the genie lowered the giant rock onto the two remaining girls killing them."

I knew the "Rocher" was more than a place to play. It was sacred to them. They accompanied me to the very top of the slippery steep rock, and I became enraptured by the magnificent panorama of the treetops and red clay earth and how the views of peace and beauty so harshly contrasted with the real-life poverty and suffering down below. The Catholic Church has honored the site with a giant rock sculpture and an altar they built with a cross above where many people from all over have made pilgrimages.

71

Figure 18 The altar on the "Rocher"

Figure 19 Jamie and Diana standing on the "Rocher" admiring
the treetop view

During the late morning of the September weekend Abidgi festival, a
few comical macho men attended the event wearing women's wigs
and make-up to prepare *foutou* for the families. They were seated on
the women's low stools with their knees up high and poked light-
hearted fun at everyone passing by, while they pounded the cassava in
large morters with giant wooden pestles that echoed throughout the
village while sipping their bangi wine. Cassava is tough and stringy
and then mixed after cooking with a bit of plantain and a touch of
palm oil. Finally, it is served in shiny rounded oval shapes in pairs
with varied sauces made of a mixture of dried or fresh fish or chicken,
eggplant, palm nuts, tomato, and carrots. At any midday, you can walk
around the village and hear the familiar banging, but during the holiday, when the families are gathered at home to celebrate with the
traditional food, the sounds from the mortars and pestles are magnified many times over. Whatever desired sauce they serve to eat with
the *foutou*, it is always spicy hot. Their piment, which is a hot
powdered spice, takes hot to a new level.

Of course, food is the high point of the weekend, but there are lots of containers filled to the brim with bangi being passed around and a spirit known as *koutoukou*, distilled to be extremely potent, which was outlawed for years because of its strength. Some of the men with glassy eyes who ramble around the village are under the *koutoukou* spell, like one of my friend Carine's brothers and also Odette's husband.

The small proportion of Muslims living in the village don't drink. They pray at their mosque in Sikensi, work hard in the fields, keep to themselves, are family men, and most originate from Burkina Faso. At one time during the 20-year presidency of Houphouet Boigny, he declared that anyone who worked on the land to make it more valuable in the Ivory Coast would be able to own that land. Many hard-working Burkinabes, usually Muslim, from neighboring Burkina Faso lived in Braffouéby to work the fields, but were not given land ownership because the land had already been divided amongst the five families who founded the village. They were not giving up their land except to their own families and they wanted and needed inexpensive labor.

Many long years ago, the five brothers left their original village of Bécédi, down the road, and came to Braffouéby to escape internal fighting. They settled there because of the natural protections from the river around the village, the smaller rocks, and the giant granite "Rocher" that they used as a post to look out for their enemies. The generations from the original five families return to the village every year to pay homage to their village and to the genies. Carine was from one of the five originals and gave me the name "Adjo." I was named after the wife of the genie protector of the village.

The Abidgis in Braffouéby and in most of the other 15 villages banned the tribal pagan ritual of entering a trance state during "dipri" when they stab their stomachs with a knife while in a trance. "Dipri is a religious, mystical and traditional celebration that dates back to the 18th century. Gomon, a village not too far away, was an exception because they insisted, "Dipri is the essence of their existence". Gomon has a population of over 8000 people and means "which exceeds human strength".

I was curious to witness the bizarre ritual located in a heavily forested zone that is performed only during the annual Abidgi weekend festival. Raymond, an unusually tall 18-year-old and the young nephew of Odette and Samuel offered to take me to Gomon. Carine clicked her tongue loudly in disapproval when I told her I was going. "Sauvages", she said shaking her head.

Sorcery was frowned upon by the Christian missionaries who made many converts in the area where the Abidgi tribe lived. There are numerous Protestant churches and one Catholic church in the village of Braffouéby, a population of only 1500. Their choral groups are especially rhythmic and inspiring, and they often sing together with neighboring villages. One mosque in Sikensi, the largest surrounding town, with about 58,000 people, serves the smaller Muslim population in the area. Most Muslims, however, reside in the northern part of the country.

Raymond went on to explain, "Gomon had split from the other villages because they chose to continue the bloody piercings of dipri while the Christians in the other villages had banned it. The missionaries called it pagan... And don't get too close to them while they are in a trance." He revealed that the people believe the ritual to be a way to summon the spirits for their purification. In the early morning the chief performs the rituals aimed at the spirits of the ancestors and the genies and he asks for health and economic prosperity. The ceremony addresses the peoples wishes and warnings about the future and ends in the chief telling people to give up their malicious ways. After his address they go to the sacred river with the ancestors for a ritual bath followed by a mask of kaolin, the clay found in the river. Water and kaolin and wearing white symbolize purity. "The cult celebrates in ceremonies of self-transcendence, purification, and rebirth while communicating to the ancient spirits asking them to put an end to religious worship and for new beginnings and reconciliation with oneself and with others." We did not witness those ceremonies about the purification but dipri means fall into the river or to wash in the river. The origin of the festival is a commemoration of the sacrifices of the founders of the tribe whose people, they promised, would soon experience abundance after living in scarcity.

Hypnotic background sounds of beating drums welcomed Raymond and me when we arrived in Gomon, after the other morning ceremonies had already taken place. The atmosphere was very still except for the drums. Along both sides of the deep red clay main street, similar to our village, the families had set up altars commemorating their ancestors on small tables or chairs covered with white fabric. Two eggs were carefully placed in front of old, framed, sepia-toned, sometimes slightly torn photographs of their honored, sullen straight-faced ancestors.

I tried not to stare when I saw one man with a bare chest wearing a short white cloth wrapped at his waist, transferring a whole egg from his mouth to the mouth of another man. Eggs, I understood, are a symbol of fertility, but I wasn't prepared for the egg-sharing scene.

One of the first women with bulging, never blinking red eyes that we observed walking around in a daze looked like she was on drugs. Dressed in a white tank top and white fabric loosely tied at her waist, she began frenetically dancing in her bare feet in circles. The drums filled the air getting louder as we neared the scene, and she whirled around still in a trance. She picked up a machete from a sun bleached wooden bench and she continued to swirl, then after slowing down, she stabbed herself in the stomach. Nobody reacted except me, since I was the only outsider on the scene. Her whirling dervish-type dance became more intense again with the drums beating faster ending in an abrupt collapse in a pool of blood. She writhed around on the earth for a few more minutes until she stood up and fled the scene.

I observed many other people staggering around in the crowds and bumping into people in their all-white blood-stained clothing, appearing to dance and at the same time be asleep with their eyes wide open. Some people had already been in a deeper trance state, and some of the others were working their way into one.

"OK, Raymond. I think I have seen enough. Let's get out of here. ASAP"

He laughed and said, "Enough?... Already?"

Figure 20 Dipri

Many children in Braffouéby are also painted with kaolin clay by their mothers when they are feeling sick. They believe it cools them and has other various health benefits and it also purifies them. Adults sometime wear it as a form of decoration or young girls wear painted designs during ceremonies.

There were many cultural practices that continued to open my eyes. The tradition was that family and friends gather for a solemn vigil, taking turns sitting by the casket to pay respects throughout the night. They erected a large structure made of bamboo trees they brought in from the forest by pounding the poles in the ground and fashioning a roof across the top with the branches for shade. The body is in a decorated with pagne and palm leaves casket at a sight elevation in the front of the newly put newly put together structure. Someone plays music from tapes and someone else plays the drums. I didn't usually last a whole night, but I could count on hearing the drumbeats or the music from a boom box with loudspeakers until daybreak.

When I first moved into the village, an elderly man from a prosperous family who had resided directly across the way from me, just passed

76

away. Janet, my sister, came for a quick visit just in time for the particularly large village funeral. A bleeding cow carcass appeared on the ground right outside my window. We didn't know if it was dead or alive until a child approached it and cautiously poked it with a nearby stick. The cow lifted his head for a couple of seconds as if to say, "What the hell is going on here?" We were spooked and both of us screamed and ran away into my house. That night we attended the family's funeral celebration. It was the most elaborate funeral of any that I ever attended, with the feasting of two cows that we chose not to eat, large amounts of bangi and African gin, live music, and dancing that lasted the entire night. I have never seen a cow again, dead or alive, in the village and that particular funeral was the largest because the departed was a "grand type", a big shot. Their very large family and many friends came in from all over Côte d'Ivoire to celebrate his life in high style, but a family member confessed to me that there wasn't enough money, however, to take him to the hospital in Abidjan. There was no healthcare in the village.

Most people could not afford the transport in an ambulance or taxi to Abidjan or to another town with a clinic. I thought about how a thriving rural village is dependent on the good health of its people, and there were too many of them with health issues, including pregnant women with only traditional midwives available with no professional healthcare training if there were complications.

My Sinking Marriage

My water broke one morning while getting ready to take my son Michael to Marshall Field's Department store in downtown Chicago to see Santa in December of 1974. I was rushed to the Hammond, Indiana, hospital when I heard the doctor say, "Your baby is losing oxygen. It's too late for a cesarean." They put me in a room for prep when during another contraction, a tiny blue leg appeared coming out of me. My ears started ringing, and I held my breath out of fear, and then screamed for my husband who was standing in the hall outside the door. He notified the nurse, and I was immediately readied and rolled into surgery. Matthew's birth date had been miscalculated. It was too early...a month early. I had attended "Prepared Childbirth" classes, but there was no preparation for a footling breach birth. Two doctors attended and cut my cervix to get him out. They put me under for the procedure with a gas mask and then gave me another gas to wake me up under an intense flashing hospital light while the nurses screamed in my face, "Push." The same process was repeated a countless number of times. It was a harsh and terrifying experience.

Matthew was a miracle baby with a full term weight of seven pounds. The doctors who delivered him, my doctor was out of town, came to my bedside while I was still groggy and said, "You would not be alive, nor would your son be alive if it was not for us." At the time, I had not yet seen my baby, and I couldn't bring myself to praise them. I had already waited what seemed like forever and just wanted to see my new baby!

I spoke softly, "I want to see my baby," and then many more times in a louder voice, "Please, bring me my baby." I became delirious.

My husband was there but he was anxious to leave and celebrate the birth of his new son at "the club" while I lay alone in bed in an acute state of anxiety. He had no idea how to comfort me, nor did he seem that concerned. All night long, I continued to beg to see my child.

"You will see your baby in 24 hours," a nurse finally revealed sometime in the middle of the night.

I was not allowed to get out of bed, was hooked up, and didn't have the strength anyway. My heart was beating erratically from the anguish, and so they gave me an EKG while I was still pleading with them to bring me, my baby.

The next day after hardly any sleep, the time had finally come to have a nurse bring Matthew in to see me. My husband was there. Matthew's little baby eyes were open wide as saucers, like he couldn't believe what he had been through. He was perfect and beautiful, and I couldn't take my own eyes off of him, insisting that he stay in my room, against their wishes.

After a week of recuperation, we all left for home. Terry and 4-1/2-year-old Michael had made a "welcome home" sign which warmed my heart after being away from him for so long. I was still an emotional, hormonal wreck. I had a breakdown screaming and sobbing when I saw my young son with a toy gun pointing at us, which Terry knew I was vehemently against.

We came home with a healthy baby. I recognize and applaud that the doctors were able to save us both and know from my own dreadful experience how childbirth is a trauma for the mother as well as for the baby.

Ivory Coast Mothers and Children, our non-profit, creates the possibility of safe childbirth for women, and I know my experience helped propel me to make labor and delivery much safer for the women in the Braffouéby region.

My husband and I took a trip on his friend's boat in Lake Erie out to Put-in-Bay during a summertime weekend away. It was a festival-like scene where multiple boats tied onto each other, and the merry-makers jumped from one boat to another to get to the park and meet and greet people along the way. Terry was acting more distant than usual, so I left the boat and walked through the crowds feeling sorry for myself and watched all the people frolicking around. I learned forty years later from a casual remark from someone who knew him that a hooker was on board while I was gone that day. What a thing to tell someone after such a long time. I had a sense that things had gone all wrong. I felt especially detached from him at the time, but I didn't know why or how to talk about it or even what to do about it. Any attempt I did make for a discussion fell on deaf ears and an empty heart.

Terry and I took a trip to Paris sometime later, when the boys were four and nine, with another couple who were madly in love with each other. It was painfully obvious how happy they were by their snuggling, giggling and continual banter about every little thing along the way.

Lara asked me after several days if I would like to have a drink with her in a café because she "wanted to have a chat."

She opened our meeting with the cutting question, "What are you doing with him?"

She proceeded to dissect the relationship that she had witnessed over the years. She told me that he was holding me back and that he was not the man for me. I could feel myself twitching inside until I blew up and strongly defended my life.

"I am very happy being married. You are out of line!" I cried. "I have been happily married for eleven years."

"You have nothing in common with him. I see how miserable you are with him time after time. When will you admit it?"

"Divorce is out of the question! I would never get a divorce!" I was adamant and started to get up from the table.

Lara then told me that she was divorced and that she went on to assure me that there was a life after. I broke down crying uncontrollably when I was faced with the truth. The truth hurt so deeply. I needed to take control of my life and knew I couldn't hide anymore.

"It's time," I muttered days later and then "I can not do this," in the next breath.

My first mission after arriving home, against the will of my husband, was to get a job. I landed a sales job in a local art gallery, where I began to come alive and build confidence in myself. I was hiding behind an "I am dumb, and I am not attractive" complex. I had never heard of the term "gaslighting," but I immediately understood the experience when it became a popular expression. I began to examine my feelings of self-doubt and confusion and I needed to get real.

I am not sure that the best way to get a grip on my life was to have a romantic affair with a handsome young Frenchman, but I took that path. He romanced me as if I had entered into a dreamscape. Fresh flowers at work, at lunch, he had a "pique-nique" packed up, ready for a rowboat ride in Lincoln Park. We would go to the ballet together or attend performance art somewhere. I weakened when I saw his bathtub in front of the roaring fireplace in his bedroom. I wished I could have gone through the process of divorce without infidelity, but I fell madly in love with him at first sight, as corny as it seems, and then ultimately, I fessed up to Terry. And I told him that I wanted a divorce.

The first thing my husband said to me after I told him was, "I knew I would lose you as soon as you walked out the door to get a job."

We stayed up all night talking until the sun came up more than we ever had before, while we both cried about the new reality. My tears were more about tears from fear.

He lost control of me. We were not a good match, and I felt little connection to him other than being the father of our children, and he was a good father because he loved his boys. I wanted to have a life that I chose and not always according to his plan. He was happy the way we were, and I was not.

To avoid another disagreement, I naively allowed that I would use the same lawyer as his and split everything we owned down the middle. I walked into the meeting before the divorce court when the lawyer immediately informed me that he would be representing Terry and not me. I knew his lawyer. He had a bully-like attitude and then he looked at me and said, "You will just have to learn to live like the rest of us." I wanted out no matter what it took and knew in the end that I would one day be free. I would pay the price.

Ten years out of the job market, I was lucky to find my job, although low paying. I had enough money to buy groceries and minimal items for my sons and for childcare.

The in-my-face loud protests from my family and my angry older son especially drove me to seek help. My own mother said, "He isn't an alcoholic. He doesn't beat you. You can't divorce him because you don't like him." Her words were blistering, but it wasn't her fault because I had never confessed to her how distraught I had been while living my "I am so happy" lie.

My own father said, "I love you more than ever and if you need anything, you come to me, but I will not talk to you during this time." His decree was harsh to hear, but I know how the Catholic church frowned upon divorce and he was a devout Catholic.

My Godfather dismissed me saying that he disowned me, but to his credit, two weeks before he died, he apologized, and I forgave him. My older sister called my boyfriend a "French gigolo" in front of the family. Most of my siblings scorned me and said that I destroyed the family, except for my brother, Nick, who quietly divorced his wife right after me, and Felix, who said that he would beat Terry up if he ever touched me, which Terry never did.

My friends stopped inviting me anywhere. For the first time, I felt completely alone except for my beloved cousin, Kathy, whose children were the same age as mine and who was my one true friend. I stayed away from my family and believed that they would all understand one day, and I told them so.

I desperately needed therapy to help me sort everything out and tell the truth. The psychologist muttered few words during my many tearful sessions until the very last time when he declared, "Your divorce is your last chance of claiming power in your life." The couch was a safe space to look myself in the eye and take charge. Even today, if I happen to smell the familiar tobacco from his incessant pipe, anxiety smacks me as if I was still sitting in his office. The powerful smell transports me back in time when I regurgitated the whole truth about my sadness and insecurities.

I brought my older son, Mike, with me to see the therapist because we were having conflicts over everything during the first years of our divorce. He was caustic and saw my weaknesses and then boldface verbally attacked me, which was never before in his character. He told me that the divorce didn't bother him, nor did he care about it ...or me, but he continually acted out. At one point, he said that I ruined his life, wouldn't touch me and that he hated me. I was devastated, completely broken-hearted. The therapist read him right away and had him sit in his impressive big black leather chair that swiveled around and gave him that sense of power and control while I mainly left them alone hoping he would get through to him.

I begged Terry to take EST with me, a 60-hour seminar over two weekends which turned out to be more of a concentrated couple's therapy for us. Both of us agreed to drop the old issues and move on, and keep our agreements with each other, and I needed to not blame others for my inadequacies or unhappiness. I started making a conscious effort to work on all of my issues and I began to take responsibility for my life and create the life I wanted. For me, it was powerful. We communicated better and soon Terry began to understand why we had to go our separate ways which was our only option. Many people disparaged the EST seminars and called it a cult, but it worked for me. We both moved on. I was determined to take charge of my life and to find a place for myself with the boys while sharing child-rearing responsibilities with my new soon to be ex-husband.

I was determined to connect with Mike again. His grades in conduct had plummeted to F's and his courses were A's. His schoolteacher met me outside her classroom one afternoon, wringing her hands and described how he had recently driven his bike down the middle of the hallway, causing havoc. She continued to lament about the gall he had that same morning to claim that our dog ate his homework. I know he belittled her in class because I heard about that at home. My biggest fear was to lose him to what horrible thing in the world, I didn't know. The only way I found to connect with him was to drive him around on Sunday mornings for his paper route with the giant bundles of heavily stuffed Chicago Tribunes. He always liked to have his own income stream and with me supporting his goal, he was happy unless, of course, it was illegal, but that is another story. I had become his target and the villain in his life, but somehow through persistence, we managed to slowly work through our differences, and he gradually became the loving, generous, and clever young man I knew him to be .

It never felt right to marry again. I never found the right person, but more importantly, I enjoyed the independence of being single, especially since I was young and immature when I married. I dated many younger men not necessarily suitable for marriage, but who I thoroughly enjoyed. I wasn't looking for a long-term relationship and I was curious about what I thought I missed during my 20s. Besides, I learned very early on that it was not a good idea to bring a man around the house in Munster, Indiana. Mike and Matt were challenging alone, but as a team against me, they were beastly. Together, they would push me to my limits because they knew I especially wanted them to be on their best behavior if I ever invited a new "friend" home. I learned the hard way to only bring someone home if it was a Sunday, Monday, or Thursday, when the boys were off at their dad's house.

If it was a Thursday night, however, I would stay in Chicago probably to meet with my youngest sister, Liz, and her friends or a friend or two I had met in the city. My new friends would often invite me to stay overnight, usually my very kind friend, Ellie, so that I wouldn't have to drive back to Indiana after one of our wild, carefree nights on the town. We were eager to immerse ourselves in the myriad of delights waiting for us in the big city.

My sons continued to taunt me and test my patience. When I started the car in the morning, the windshield wipers were turned on at full blast to greet me, along with the heater and the radio on their hard rock station. After work when I drove up our driveway at home to the "River", as the boys called it, with my headlights shining in the living room window, I could often see the frenzied activity of young boys and girls moving back and forth in a race to hide whatever they were doing. Upon entering the living room after they had installed themselves properly in the furniture, I was greeted by a chorus of "Hello, Mrs. Mertz," reminding me of the polite Eddie Haskell character types. Admittedly, I gave my sons a long leash and I enjoyed their friends and liked to engage with them, as was demonstrated by my own parents.

My two sons' most flagrant misdeeds were when I walked in one night after my long grueling commute on the Dan Ryan expressway to find illegal driver's licenses being issued and sold in my living room. They argued as if it was a sanctioned business and that I should not close it down because they were making money! Another time, an entire professional craps table for gambling was installed over the dining room table. They were so very proud of the quality of their craftsmanship. I prayed that neither one of them would ever be arrested. If it weren't for baseball, basketball, hockey, swimming, golf, and tennis, and especially their saintly coaches and disciplined teammates, I am sure that they would have wandered into even more dangerous territories.

Adding to my "divorced and working mother" suburban life, on Christmas morning, I received an unwelcome gift from my brother, Felix, who gave me and every one of my six siblings either a tarantula, a pair of rabbits, a cat, a parrot or gerbils. We were the not-so-fortunate ones to receive a puppy we named Chip, who grew into being what appeared to be the largest-sized collie ever born. Caring for the rambunctious boundary-pushing Mike and Matt was one thing, but a big new hairy puppy that desperately needed to be trained was a whole other can of worms, and by the way, the dog had worms on that same memorable Christmas morn.

Chip, the dog, soon garnered a rap sheet with the Munster police department. The three of us were to appear in court on Michael's 11th birthday to hear the evidence and face the judge. I wanted both boys to learn the seriousness of carelessly leaving the door open and letting the dog run free, so I insisted that they go with me. At the last minute, Matthew was feeling sick, and he did indeed feel warm. I thought since the police station was located down the street from us, I left Matthew, age 7, home alone.

The judge read the grievances against our dog that included trespassing on the school property, and child molesting, among other infractions that I didn't hear. My mind shut down when I heard "child molesting." I was required to pay a hefty fine and Mike learned a small lesson about consequences, as he was hyper-conscious about anything concerning money.

When we arrived home, Matthew's temperature had shot up to 104 degrees. He was hysterically crying out in panic that he saw "a bunch of people" walking outside around the house carrying knives. I immediately called the police and then my father, who all rushed over, arriving at about the same time. Nobody saw footprints in the light snow on the mud-packed late spring earth, which left the cops and my dad doubting Matthew's story.

"There is no evidence, Ma'am," said the cops.

"Matthew has been hallucinating," concluded my dad.

Since it was Mike's birthday, dad invited us all out to dinner with my parents and their friends at their favorite place, "Taco Real," while Matthew slept in the booth next to me with his sweet little head on my lap after a good dose of Tylenol. Mike became fully engrossed in the adult conversations that he usually enjoyed with his myriad of questions while Matthew slept.

Years later, the "bad dog" was redeemed and considered a hero by many of the neighbors because his barking was credited with stopping two different neighborhood burglaries. Chip died from kidney failure and refused to eat. Mike came home to buy him a deli sandwich when I alerted him that Chip was gravely ill, and he still would not eat. It was the only time Mike ever came home from the university besides Christmas. I interpreted it as "I am so happy he loves school" instead of "Why doesn't he ever come home to see his poor old mother?" I heard a few complaints like the latter.

I spent as much time as I could with my parents after the divorce when our relationship returned back to normal because I felt that their influence on the boys was important for their overall development. "Integrity" was one of my father's favorite words and I liked how he engaged with them on history, world politics and general knowledge. Mother was always delighted to see us stop in to "Knickerbocker," their home, where there was instantly enough dinner coming out of the kitchen for all of us. The boys liked to bury their noses in one of the Encyclopedia Britannicas if they weren't interrogating my father. And dad always told me to be sure and fill up my tank with gas at the corner station where he had an account, which was greatly appreciated.

Figure 21 Mike and Matt

I was nervous and shaking during my first interview with the unpretentious convivial Director of Purchasing at NBC-TV and Radio for an opportunity to work in the thriving and storied Merchandise Mart. I sat across from him at his massive-sized desk scattered with stacks of papers for almost an hour that seemed more like a conversation at somebody's kitchen table rather than an intimidating, inquisition-like interview so I began to relax a bit.

Ready to wrap it up and feeling confident, since he didn't seem to feel any sense of urgency, I blurted out, "Well, did I get the job?"

He responded with a deep belly laugh. I had no idea that a person had to pass through the ranks that included many levels before being hired to work for the large RCA owned corporation. I did finally get the job, but he would often say, "Why did I hire you, Miss Pat? You don't know how to type."

I had bigger stars in my eyes years later during my grand tour and interview at NBC at 30 Rockefeller Plaza. The position was what I had always dreamed about and had prepared for by taking classes at a Chicago business school that offered Purchasing Management courses, courtesy of NBC. Sadly, it was not to be. The boys firmly stated they would live with their dad if I moved to New York, which was never going to happen. I turned down the big job because I would not leave Chicago without them.

I began calculating my next move. What kid wouldn't want to live in California? I set up an interview in Burbank and packed my bags. My agenda included meeting a good friend of my younger brother Felix who I had reacquainted with at my brother's wedding and who was finishing his degree at USC. I was yearning for a break.

I was met at the airport by Terrible, as he became known, dressed to kill, driving a shiny new car. He invited me to Catalina Island to dive for abalone but stopped first to buy me a wet suit. And off we went in a glass helicopter where we spotted a whale swimming along below in the sparkling blue Pacific Ocean.

I felt especially sexy in my slick black catsuit as we frolicked in the crystal clear cool water to search for the rough grey shells with the pearly insides. There was an abundance of abalone and we scooped up as many as we could carry. Terrible was his gallant and polite self in an overly exaggerated manner.

Next on his agenda was a trip up the "mountain" towards the center of the island to find wild buffalos that were supposedly roaming around. He rented a bright-colored open-air jeep to climb up the road, where we came upon a young couple holding hands along side a fence. He stopped the car, chatted them up and offered them a ride upon discovering that they were newlyweds. They immediately hopped in and cozied up to each other in the back seat.

It was impossible not to notice the "No Trespassing" signs posted everywhere. We approached a gate with a sign that clearly stated that we were on private property. Ignoring the signs, he drove around the gate and continued up the winding road prompting the nervous newlyweds to hop out with a quick goodbye. I began to express caution myself and was not feeling the same fervor to "find the buffalos" as he was. Sure enough, I glanced over to find a flashing light on top of a dark blue car that was arriving at breakneck speed behind us. They brought us down to the station and ushered him into a room and closed the door. I was ordered to sit on a cold hard chair in the waiting room. After a while, I noticed a ticker tape of sorts that was printing out a very long paper back and forth behind the giant front desk. The machine continued the clicking sounds for what seemed like forever.

A plump older woman with a high ponytail seated behind the desk was watching the machine. I delicately approached her and inquired, "Would all that information being spouted out right now perhaps pertain to my friend?'

Her eyes looked up at me without moving her head. "Yes."

"I see, thank you."

Hours later, he emerged. We traveled back, not saying much because he realized there would be thousands of dollars in attorney fees and a court appearance in the future.

"I need to get to Burbank," I reminded him.

"Let's get out of here." He responded.

He warned me that he had to run an errand early the next morning, which would take an hour or so.

"OK. I need to take some time to make myself look professional, anyway."

On the way to the rental car office back on home turf, I was ready to go. He stopped the car and got out. I became curious as to why he was fussing with something in the trunk for so long, only for me to exit the car and discover that it was fully loaded with blocks of cocaine.

"Oh, Uh huh. I see"

I rented a car and arrived very late for my interview in a flop sweat for a ride that should have taken only an hour and a half. My map was not of highest quality and I could not understand the highway system with all of the traffic and the speeding cars and the signs and turn-offs that said: "In the direction of blah blah." I did not know what cities were near my destination to understand the "direction." What was wrong with the Midwest way of saying "north, south, east, or west?" I got lost and hated all the driving. I found Burbank to be unattractive, and I was exasperated and exhausted.

I didn't push it when Mike and Matt said in unison, "I am not moving to California."

My seven years at NBC-TV and Radio, Chicago, with over 600 employees, its lively culture and toxic masculinity in the '80s, ended when I declined their generous offer to relocate. Little did I know that I was at the very onset of their enormous downsizing process after the parent company, RCA, sold out to General Electric. They went from 600 employees to under 80.

My last day on Halloween afternoon, in costume, I wore a vintage full-length chenille robe with a large colorful peacock emblazoned on the back. I was laid off by Raggedy Ann. The head of Human Resources was in full array with bright red lipstick, and red triangle nose, wearing red striped legs, red yarn hair, and a white starched apron, while I sat in her office to hear about my fate. Instantly, my head started to spin when I heard the details of my "lay-off." I left her office, attempting to assimilate my new reality learned from a doll I used to play with as a child, and proceeded to walk down the long corridor through a haze of flashing lights towards the Purchasing Department to clear out my desk.

A few doors down from HR, the nurse's station beckoned me. I stumbled through the door and then crashed into a shelf filled with medical supplies and fell to the floor. After the nurse helped me up, she lead me to a bed, and had me lie down. Someone later came in from security to officially accompany me to my office and to gather up my personal possessions. I caught sight of the spindle on my desk, heavily stacked with pink "While You Were Out" urgent messages that suddenly didn't mean a damn thing. My career path at NBC as "Purchasing Pat" was over.

I became a "job-hopper," attempting advertising sales, health insurance sales, direct marketing sales, Cadillac sales, Personal Shopper at Saks Fifth Avenue, Concierge at three Chicago hotels, and eventually, Concierge/Event Planner at Goldman Sachs. Some of my career choices were better than others. My resume never contained the full information, or they would have sent me to an insane asylum.

The worst idea I had was to sell insurance. I should have listened to my dad, who let me know right away, "Nobody wants to talk to someone who sells insurance."

Tied for the worst job was buying an expensive direct mail marketing franchise sold by a fast-talking skilled salesman who made grand promises of great fortune. I spent most of my severance package from NBC and went into serious debt. One evening I came home stressed out from grinding people all day selling direct marketing coupons working for my franchise, driving all over the place, and waiting for the clients to show up to sell, approve their ads, deliver invoices, or collect money. My territory was falling into financial collapse because of the economy, and the shuttered doors that greeted me trying to collect money often meant that their buying an ad was a last futile attempt to save their failing business.

Upon walking in the door one night, cranky and wrung out at the end of another long day, Matthew was standing in the middle of the living room, yelling at the top of his lungs, "I hate Money Mailer."

I looked at him and said, "You know what? So do I."

I quit that evening and spent many years paying back the bank for my franchise loan. I was guilty of never thoroughly researching my desig-nated sales territory. The three areas where I was supposed to work were near my home, and I figured that I would just make it work since I would be closer to home for the boys.

The hotel business fascinated me because of the various challenges of a large team performing different functions and working in synch to make it all appear effortless. I first became enthralled with the idea of being a concierge back when I was married. Terry and I came to Chicago for a Saturday night stay to meet his college friends, Mike and his girlfriend, Lara. We stayed at the Whitehall Hotel. I had pre-arranged with the concierge to obtain King Tut tickets at the Field Museum. When we arrived, the tickets were not there because they had been given to another guest with the same name, Mike Murray. The hotel called the concierge at home, who had the day off. Horrified at the mix-up, she came in and personally escorted us to the museum to the front of the line making sure we were seamlessly admitted, VIP style. I was impressed and thought that would be a great position someday.

When the Gulf War started, sales plummeted at Saks Fifth Avenue. Consumerism and extra fancy clothes reflected in the TV show Dynasty with Joan Collins was ending. The store was empty, and I had grown weary and bored. My youngest sister, Liz, had been hired in the sales department to help open the new hotel, Embassy Suites State Street. Aware of my ennui and my fascination with being a concierge in a hotel, she called me at work one afternoon to say that the concierge that they hired had just left.

"Get over here now!"

I walked off the floor at that moment and showed up for an interview and was hired on the spot. There were no computers to help with directions, theatre and sports tickets, or the latest news concerning local events. I didn't have a florist, a limo company, or a ticket broker. Everything was new, except I did know a lot about the nightlife and restaurants. *The Reader*, the *Chicago Tribune* and *Where* were concierge bibles, I learned. Besides tips, we made extra cash off ticket sales (thank you, Michael Jordan, great Chicago theatre, and the Chicago Cubs), and also commissions on flowers and limousines. I would often take a turn as Manager on Duty and spend the night in the hotel and have meals at Papagus, the delicious Greek restaurant located within the hotel. My son, Matt, would come and have dinner and stay over with me sometimes when he was home from college, which was a treat.

I was soon offered a position at the Ritz Carlton concierge desk during my time at the Embassy Suites, and they required an all-day detailed training session before starting. However, I was leaving for Bora Bora the next day for two weeks with a childhood friend and my head was not readily tracking all their mind-blowing policies and procedures that I was supposed to retain, because I had already mentally checked out in anticipation of the glorious trip.

Skip, my friend, made five visits to the dreamy far-off island and was anxious for me to meet the family at Pauline's resort and experience the island's exotic beauty. I had never traveled or had been out with him anywhere before, but our parents were good friends, and I had known him my entire life. Right before we landed during our trip, he warned me that he had his own agenda on the island and that I would have my own place, and that I was to find my own way around. I had absolutely no issues with following his mandate.

Skip and I were warmly greeted at Chez Pauline by Pauline herself, accompanied by stunning women dressed in hot pink and green flowered pareo wraps, with a bright flower tucked behind each woman's ear. Skip's thatch-covered hut, located directly on the beach, had a large handwritten welcome sign enumerating all the dates he had stayed there over the years. My little "hut" was a lovely full-size bungalow with a screened-in porch on the beach at the far end of the property, directly on the lagoon of the blissful sparkling, turquoise-colored South Pacific Ocean. Deep pink hibiscus blooms were left everywhere in the house to greet me, on my pillows and in the bathroom. I knew I had found heaven on earth with the most gracious people I had ever met.

On our first night, Skip mentioned that I was hosting a big party. The owner's handsome, deeply tanned, and Tahiti-styled tattooed son, who never wore a shirt, entered my place later that evening. I was smitten. He brought the "Party Pat" out of me. We cranked up the music and danced and carried on until the wee small hours.

One of the women who worked at Chez Pauline, dressed me up in a pareo the next morning, complete with a flower in my hair. There is an art in tying the pareo just right. "Man of the Sea" arrived in his pirogue. He landed on the beach in front of my bungalow to scoop me up for an adventure on a motu, one of the very small uninhabited islands. He was strong and agile and showed off his muscles and climbing skills as he scaled all the way to the top of a coconut tree to grab a perfectly ripened fruit for us to enjoy. He was all the scenery I wanted.

Early the next afternoon, I looked out my screened-in porch to see my man with a couple of his native friends gliding up to my beach to invite me to paddle out with them for a swim with the lemon sharks. Afterward, one of them speared a tuna, brought it on board, cut it up and passed it around to eat with a bit of fresh lemon for a sushi feast. I was soon feeling loved like a Polynesian princess... and very native.

Skip and I originally had plans to visit the other islands like Moorea and maybe Rangiroa, but I begged him to stay on Bora Bora for another week because there was so much more to do and enjoy right there. My family always says, "Don't leave a great time to go and find another good time." The night that we made the decision to remain, the curtain came crashing down.

There was a luau every night with torches and dancers at the grand Hotel Bora Bora, where my friend, "Man of the Sea," knew everyone who worked there. When we arrived, his friends greeted us with pretty, fruity, boozy drinks, and we were ushered over to a private section tucked near the bar with a view of the tourists and the stage. My date began pounding cocktails and shots at an unusual rate that I had never witnessed in him before and soon he became extremely intoxicated. I saw an angry, ugly side of him of which I wanted no part. I left the party with one of his friends, who paddled me back home in his pirogue. Subsequently, I banished "Man of the Sea" from my place forever.

The next day I took off for a melancholy walk out to the point of the island near the mountains to grieve my "break-up." I noticed a clearing on the side of the road, where a very tall stunning native man with long black wavy hair and a bright warm smile was standing. He was wearing no shirt and was covered in the signature Tahitian-styled tattoos. There is something about tanned skin and a smooth, toned chest that gets me every time. I continued my walk along the unpaved road lined with tropical trees and shrubs, hoping to catch another glimpse of him somewhere on my way back.

Et le voila! Man of the Mountain was waiting for me very close to where I first saw him near the bend in the road, standing with a bright, broad smile. He held out his hand. I placed mine in his, and off we went down the path to the beach where he lived in a small house next to his family. I didn't realize so many people had homes along the shore. Some were in shambles, while others were in tidy, well-groomed areas. He told me about his family pearl business that has been in operation for decades. I left his place feeling a glow all over, anticipating our next encounter later that night.

My new handsome island man picked me up at my place on his motor-cycle before sunset and I couldn't wait to wrap my arms around his waist. We went off to a lively local inland spot with a "great jukebox" that he was anxious to show off. He carefully made his selections of song choices, and we sipped our cold Hinano beers while I was also drinking in his twinkling, soulful eyes. I floated towards him when he stood up and reached out for me to lead me to the dance floor. I was ablaze by his touch and the sensual island music, an innovative mix of reggae, calypso, and Hawaiian. It was getting late, and although I could have swayed to the rhythms in his arms forever, it was time for him to take me home. I hopped on the back of his bike, taking in one more glance over my shoulder at our dreamy island bar. Back in the dark shadows of the parking lot, I spotted the enraged "Man of the Sea" waiting for us. Our dreamy moments erupted into fury. Both men began hurling insults at each other in Tahitian. I pleaded with my former crazed friend to go away as I hung on tightly to my new man.

We sped off in a fury on the loose gravel with our aggressor trailing closely behind, but we spun out and crashed to the ground. "Man of the Mountain" was fine, but my entire leg was scraped bloody. Through my tears, I begged "Man of the Sea" to leave us alone. He eventually took off in a swirl of gravel, still hollering more crass-sounding words that echoed behind him in the soft night air. The last time that I was with "Man of the Mountain," he surprised me with a gift-wrapped tape recording of the songs he played for me from the jukebox that night to take home with me and to always remember him. I never unwrapped the gift because of my sudden departure from the island, but I still keep it in my treasures.

It was early morning at his home, and he had taken off to get us some coffee. I was relaxing, wrapped in my reveries, when I heard a frantic banging on the door by someone loudly asking for my whereabouts and then informing me that my flight was leaving in half an hour.

I had to be on that particular flight to make all the connections from Bora to Tahiti to LA and then Chicago to be able to start my new job on time. Since nobody at the Ritz was very happy in the first place that I had taken a two-week vacation after my training, there was no wiggle room. I scrambled frantically to pull myself together and arrived at the mini airport in groundbreaking speed, leaving many things behind, out of breath, and without having a moment to say goodbye or thank you to anyone, even Skip. "Man of the Mountain" would return home to an empty place.

I made it to work on time to start my new concierge position, but inwardly longed to be on my island paradise. I was tan, thin from eating only rice and fish, crippled from my bruised leg, and rocking my too-blonde, "Bora-Bora Blonde" hair, as my hairdresser called it.

How could I ever adjust to this new arrogant concierge partner who I was assigned to work with in the evenings who rolled her eyes and looked down at me in self-importance?

"This is the fax machine. This is the copy machine," I was informed pompously. OK, so I didn't know.

I was scrutinized in almost every interaction with guests. Someone from management would stand nearby and write things down and listen to conversations with guests which was uncomfortable and stifling. The Ritz had been chosen as the #1 hotel in the world. The negative atmosphere was incongruous. I gave service "above and beyond," in my estimation, which was our concierge credo, but I was baffled in believing that this was how I chose to make a living.

Over a year later, my mother, at age 73, received the devastating news that she was dying of gall bladder cancer that had metastasized. I had traveled with her to Mayo Clinic, where they determined that because of her heartburn, she was told to take Zantac in the morning, which was sadly, a misdiagnosis. My dad was already suffering from several strokes, and so I left my job at the Ritz to live with them during this unimaginable time of need and grief. My siblings were in and out on the weekends to help with the caregiving. Mike, my son, was living and working like a maniac in Chicago after his graduation with honors from the IU Business School, and Matt was still at Indiana University. I had the duty and honor of my life to stay with my parents for a year and a half.

Mother was stoic and courageous as ever since she came from the school of "We all have our little aches and pains." Dad was, for the most part, overmedicated, which took away some of his indomitable spirit but never his sense of humor.

One afternoon, my frail-looking mother, who once was so elegant and full of life but still beautiful as ever, was lying down for a nap. She reached out to me with her thin, bony hand and looked intensely into my eyes.

She said, "Patsy, will you promise me that you will one day go to Africa?"

"Why, yes," I said, my mind darting to the continent of which I knew nothing about, "Of course, I will." In Geography class during grade school, when we came to the chapters on Africa, we skipped over the pages. They called it the "Dark Continent."

Mother planted the seed and was very good at planting seeds without being instructive. She wanted me to have an African experience, I knew, something like she and dad enjoyed while on safari years before in Kenya and Tanzania. I felt she also had left a few subtle messages about her love for the people she had met in Africa when she decorated my room at the family Lake Michigan house with framed photos of the Masai Mara from their trip, wooden carved statues of wild animals and bedspreads inspired by West African mud cloth.

Mother's health began to fail fast. My six siblings came over to take turns every night to sit up with her as she lay very still. The kind women from Hospice were coming in regularly who, at first, mother had rebuked, even though she was in the founding group who had organized Hospice in the area. I was terrified of losing her and I had never before witnessed death. There was no solace, as kind and tuned in as my friends Melinda and Bruce were to me during that time. They both were so indulgent with me because all I wanted to do was talk about my mother and cry, and for that I will always be grateful.

It was time for her to go, I knew. After many long days and nights, her seven children were together with her in the room, standing around her bed. We felt the same extraordinary sensation when it happened. It was like a "poof," and then her life was gone. Being at her side with the remains after her spirit ascended to the heavens was shattering even though I knew in my mind that the day was coming. She was deeply loved by me and treasured by many and I could not imagine a life without her. And her spirit lives on!

While the bagpipes were playing solemnly at the entrance of the church before mother's funeral mass, I stood off to the side of the front door by myself, isolated and caught up in a new reality of living without my mother. My family was already seated in the front pews inside. A woman about my mother's age approached me. She was all decorated in her fancy clothes and I slightly recognized her as she stood facing me, looking me over, assessing me with her head sharply moving up and down. She then pronounced, "You will never be half the woman that your mother was." She clicked her heels, turned away and then abruptly walked through the door of the church. As mean, ugly and rude as it was for her to make a remark like that to me during my time of grief, or any time, for that matter, I knew that there was a ring of truth in it. How did she know that I had a fear of not ever being a good enough example to my sons or anything about my ongoing doubts about ever finding my way in the world?

Years later, my dear father passed away in his sleep after many strokes and many days and weekends spent caring for him, enjoying his larger-than-life sparkle and his love. I hold dear the memory of how his face would light up with his bright smile and how his slumped-over body suddenly lost 20 years whenever I visited on the weekends to stay with him at his lake house. I would miss him, his wit and wisdom forever.

Before he died, he made two sad memories disappear. One was that he knew that he wasn't there emotionally for my mother when she was nearing her death. His love and sharp sense of humor were a deep bond they shared. I held dear the memories of their long-time magical relationship that set a standard for me. He was capable of giving her more, even after being handicapped by multiple strokes and too many meds. He admitted that he failed her when he should have tried to comfort her. His words hit me hard because it was the truth. He wasn't the type to express deep feelings very often, but he told me how much he loved her and that he let her down. We cried together.

The second thing he said was that he was sorry that at every one of my birthdays, he would tell the same story of how I was supposed to be a boy and was to be born on his father's birthday, October 12th. I was a girl and was born on October 11th at 11 PM. He thought that was a funny story. I wondered from a young age if they ever wanted me to be born and if I was a disappointment. In fact, I hated that story because I felt I had let him down. He admitted after so many years, "I am sorry for telling that story every year," and then he said that he loved me and was very happy and proud to have me as his daughter. He was an extraordinary, good, kind and highly respected man of faith, country, and family. He was my hero.

After both of my parents had departed, there were some rough times ahead getting along with my three brothers and three sisters. I came to realize how much of a peacemaker my mother was from behind the scenes. Somehow, we made it through the storms and presently, we all (their twenty grandchildren and their seven children) get along just like my parents had always advocated. We learned to either work it out or let it go. In the words of my dear wise mother, it is always best to "rise above it."

My parents gave me courage and strength through their exemplary lives of giving not only financial resources but also their time and their talents. And when they were gone, it was up to me to create my own legacy. It was clear. The "chatter" in my head was that I was not capable, but I could no longer hide behind either one of my departed parents. I knew I would have to embrace the chatter and hopefully move forward with something worthwhile, whatever it was.

Life Altering Message

There would usually be a wait after I rushed to be on time for a meeting or to watch choral practice, or observe the women's literacy classes in Braffouéby, always trying my best to learn more about the culture. I would take deep breaths and tell myself to be in the moment, be conscious, and take it all in or any other crazy thing to

101

calm myself down. I had to keep in mind that nobody had watches or clocks but knew to arrive when they were ready in the evenings after their chores were finished. There was "American time" and "African time," which the teacher of the class who knew the difference and he explained it to me in a playful manner.

The literacy classes were well attended on Tuesday evenings in the village where they were learning how to read and write in Abidgi because many girls had dropped out of school. The women were genuinely happy to see me there, but never let on about the fact that they didn't understand me very well because most, I later realized, did not attend enough school to learn French. My Abidgi language skills were limited to the perfunctory polite everyday dialogs. I enjoyed being with the women as an opportunity to communicate about HIV/AIDS and savor the joy they manifested by simply being there together.

The women had no problem understanding my presentations when I passed around packs of rubbers with my extra-large black wooden penis. The women started tittering in embarrassed laughter while they practiced placing the rubber on the phallus. My first job was to help prevent the spread and the fear associated with HIV/AIDS and help eliminate the stigma, which we spent a lot of time focused on during our training.

The Peace Corps office in Abidjan gave us information as to where we could find boxes of rubbers at no cost to distribute in our villages. The word was out that I had the goods, and I did my best to stock the little village "boutiques" with the rubbers where they sold palm oil, salt, sugar, and sometimes soft drinks. The product flew off the shelves. I often would hear a knock on my door in the middle of the night when the boutiques ran out of product from some man looking for protec-tion, *"Pardon, Madame Patricia, pardon. Excusez-moi. Vous avez les capotes?"*

It is customary but not required during the service of a Peace Corps volunteer to develop a sustainable project besides whatever you agreed to do as your job and talk about HIV/AIDS. Our active village community group decided they wanted to raise *agouti*, much to my chagrin since they were ugly, rat-like mini beasts. The rodents used to be plentiful in the wild, but because of population growth, most of them were hunted and killed. I didn't like the way they looked or tasted, but it was not about what I wanted; it was about what they wanted. I recalled my initial encounter with *agouti* at the home of my host family and shivered all over at the thought of raising them. It was time to tell the Chief of the village since I had already sent N'Guessen to an *agouti*-raising school from funding that I gathered from my kind son Mike and dear brother Pete. I was eager to set up a meeting with the Chief to brief him about our progress and about how close we were to the reality of having an *agouti* farm.

Before I was able to make my full presentation, the chief interrupted with, "The village needs a clinic."

At first, I went numb because there was no way, I thought, that I could ever do anything of such grandiosity.

"And what about the *agouti* project we all have been planning?" I whispered disappointedly.

I learned early on that it was not possible to argue with the chief. He had a very commanding presence, spoke beautiful French, was a bit misogynistic but he was the authority, the last word, end of argument. He was the chief. And he was kind.

"When school starts in a couple of weeks, the children, along with the teachers, are geared up to build a garden for *agouti* food," I gushed while attempting to ignore what he declared.

The Chief cut me off again and proceeded to tell me the heart-wrenching story about his daughter.

"When my daughter, Marie Claire, went into labor in the middle of the night, my family put her in a wheelbarrow, and since there are no lights, cars, or taxis in the village, they pushed her down the long dark, bumpy road to Bécédi to find help. Her baby died on the way, and she was seriously injured during delivery and almost bled to death."

I was dumbstruck. There was nothing more to say. The idea of building a clinic was way out of the realm of possibilities for me and way beyond my comfort zone. I tried my best to forget their story, but I could not. I soon realized that her experience was probably not the only one like it.

My Sister Janet

Soon after my *agouti* confrontation with the Chief, I received the welcome news that my sister, Janet, was coming for another visit on her way back from South Africa, where she was working with an international organization. Ivory Coast was hardly on the way, but the fact that she was going to make such a grand detour again, I wanted to surprise her with a party I named "Fête de Janette." I would plan a welcome for her with all the traditional fanfare available. For entertainment, I would invite the famed dancers from the neighboring village of Bécédi and feast on macaroni, (the only pasta available which is really spaghetti) and order bottles of bangi wine and invite all the neighbors. I informed the chief that she was arriving and about my party plans.

The chief shook his head and declared, "You have not given me enough time to be able to protect our village from evil spirits! No, it is impossible to bring in people from Bécédi."

He explained that there had to be a village meeting with enough time beforehand when the men do whatever it is that they do to avert an "inevitable disaster." How that happened, I was not privy. All I really understood at the moment was the word *"non."*

With both eyes fixated on me, he warned, "If someone died, it would be your fault."

OK, I knew he was serious, as usual, and I followed his orders. People were dying all the time and I didn't want to be held responsible for any more deaths. As a solution, my good friend, Carine, arranged to have the same dancers in Bécédi perform for us in their village, complete with drumbeats, dancers, and rhythmic instruments. She also invited us both over to her restaurant maquis for an Ivorian feast with traditional favorites. The altered party plans were coming together thanks to Carine.

I was admitted to the Peace Corps infirmary for the umpteenth time with stomach problems and I was looking forward to recovery and welcoming Janet, who was arriving in Abidjan at the end of my infirmary stay. A spider bit me again, this time, as I was leaving the village. By the time I arrived in Abidjan at the health center, the volunteers called "Club Med", my foot was swollen and throbbing, beet red. The nurse treated it and at the end of the treatment, she placed a black rock on the wound. So, I don't really know what worked, the treatment or the black rock, just like the traditional medicine in the village.

When I was feeling better on the morning Janet was arriving, I decided to venture out and get a long overdue pedicure at a salon not far from the Peace Corps Infirmary. On my way back from the salon, I chose to take a shortcut over a wide-open field with tall grass in some areas next to a large, impoverished encampment with corrugated tin roofs where children attended school and people lived. The field was open for a reason. Unbeknownst to me, it was the depository of their raw sewage. Halfway through the "field," I began sinking into a muddy morass, and I could not get out.

"Is this quicksand? What is going on?" I yelled to nobody.

I began screaming for help, *"Au secours, au secours."*

A middle-aged stranger in a sun bleached torn shirt finally appeared from the dwelling. He stood there with his hands on his hips for what seemed like forever, gawking at me and shaking his head in disbelief.

Finally, he leaned over with a long stick he found nearby to pull me out and all the while, he kept repeating the same question, "What are you doing in there?"

I didn't know the word for a shortcut, and I was much too distressed and immobilized to explain to him that I thought it was an open field.

"Je ne sais pas" was the easiest thing to say. "I don't know!" I cried countless times.

I had lost my flip-flops in the deep wet muck and was worried about bacteria getting into a cut from the pedicure. I hung on to that long stick for dear life and I finally managed to lift each leg high enough, taking labored steps to reach solid ground. I thanked him for saving me, but he was annoyed and angry to find an outsider on his property and continued to shake his head in disbelief.

I slogged back to the infirmary in my bare feet on the pebbly ground scattered with miscellaneous debris, knowing I was covered in e coli, salmonella and every other bacterium known and unknown to mankind. I scrubbed myself in the shower with detergents until my skin was raw. "Was this a metaphor for my life?" I thought the worst. I had found a savior who wanted nothing to do with me while I was slowly sinking away deep in despair from my ignorance and stomach aches. Janet was just the tonic I needed.

I was embarrassed and chose not to tell anyone at the infirmary. Janet was soon to arrive and had been ironically attending an Infection Prevention meeting in Johannesburg.

We met at the airport without a hitch and headed back to Braffouéby in a taxicab. It felt luxurious for me to be in a cab instead of a bus at the reviled Adjamé bus station. There were a few problems with the transport, however. There happened to be a large hole in the floorboard of the car, and we were able to see the road below. There were no working headlights or windshield wipers as it started to rain and it was getting dark after we left the highway toward the village. Janet was visibly upset. The reason the driver kept opening the door and looking out was that he was checking his tire. Without pulling over to the side of the road, he came to a complete stop in the middle of a pitch-black road and he left the car. We soon learned he had stopped to find a tool from a dwelling nearby to change the tire. He had no flashing warning lights on the cab, and Janet just about flipped out at that point. We could have been hit from behind on the narrow road, but it always seemed to me that African eyes see better in the dark than Western eyes. I tried to reason with her. I am not willing to say if our experience in a taxi was better or worse than catching a bus at Adjamé. I was a true believer in Guardian Angels.

Janet's multiple suitcases were loaded with presents for everyone in typical generous Janet fashion. She bought bags of candy for all the children in the village at the Sikensi market, which our welcome committee, composed of children, spotted right away. They worked themselves into a frenzy to get their hands on some of the "bonbons". Word traveled at breakneck speed about the lollipops that she eventually handed out, and before I knew it, there were large swarms of children screaming and rioting outside my door with their outstretched hands coming in from all directions squealing for some "bonbons." Equally as fast, one of the women elders appeared in the courtyard to reprimand us, saying, "Never, ever do that again!" The children scattered at the sight of her with good reason. The women mean business and the children know it.

Janet bought some new flip-flops for herself when we visited the market to stock up on provisions, but she noticed that Sahara wasn't wearing any shoes at all. Janet let her wear her new ones, but didn't have the heart to take them away from her when we arrived home. Sahara flashed Janet her million dollar smile that was nothing short of pure glee and gratitude.

How delighted was I to learn that my sister had also tucked away inside her overstuffed suitcases some gorgeous wines that she brought from the South African vineyards for us to enjoy? I was looking forward to my 8 PM door-closing time to dive into some of that heavenly bon vin more than ever. We both became a little tipsy that night and laughed and told stories until very late. It was a welcome respite after some very challenging days and weeks, and months.

I convinced Janet to fly home from Ghana rather than return to Abidjan to catch her flight so that she would be able to delight in the beaches, speak English, and experience a whole other African culture and quite frankly, I loved Ghana. She agreed. I checked to make sure that we had a decent car without a hole in the floorboard and arranged for someone to take us to the border where we could easily find transport to our destination. As we were driving away, all loaded up with Janet's bags and my backpack, leaving empty wine bottles and the *agouti* raising money hidden behind in the house, and the microfinancing project savings from the women, we headed towards the familiar bumpy road leading us out of the village. There was a crowd of young children who ran after our car waving, wishing us well and saying goodbye. We leaned our heads out the window and blew kisses to them while they squealed with delight. The image of those children is emblazoned deep in my heart. Little did I know that was the last time I was ever to see them again as little children in Braffouéby and as a Peace Corps volunteer.

We were soon settled in a most beautiful 4-star hotel in Elmina on the beach near Cape Coast, Ghana. Janet rose early and headed to the shower, and I luxuriated a bit longer between the clean crisp pressed sheets while contemplating the all-important decision of whether we should have room service or just watch TV.

The night before, we met some Ghanaians who I had encountered on the beach during a previous trip to the Cape Coast with my Peace Corps cronies. They remembered my name, or because they called me "mama," I answered them because of their warm welcome, complete with outstretched arms. After my favorite Ghanaian dinner of peanut chicken with rice and beers, Janet and I joined the beach party in front of the hotel where we all sat around a giant campfire that they built to resemble a towering skyscraper accompanied by guitar music and a medley of songs. When the young Rastas lit the fire, I recalled one of the many reasons why I wanted to return to that same beach. It was a spectacular sight to see the blazing towering inferno. I requested the song "Oh Cecelia, You're Breakin' My Heart" because I had just heard the news that my dear nephew, Gary Robert and his beautiful wife, Lisa, just had their first new baby girl who they named Cecelia. It was a dreamy night on the sand by the sea with my sister and the lively, warm group of Ghanaians. Did I have some *gangia*? Of course, I did.

That next morning my face still had a smile on it while relaxing and reflecting on the previous evening. I rolled over and reached for the remote control and turned on the TV. A developing news flash blasted across the screen, revealing that there had been a coup d'état in Côte d'Ivoire, with bloodshed all over the north and in the capital city of Abidjan. My heart sank to the floor.

"I should be there in the village with the Ivorians," I cried out to Janet in the shower, who couldn't hear me and hadn't heard the news yet, but I already knew that it would be impossible.

When I finally reached our Country Director by telephone, he said to stay where I was and that all the 130 volunteers would be evacuated as soon as possible to Ghana.

Janet made every effort to convince me to leave with her on her flight. "Let's fly to Ireland! Let me take you to Paris?" Janet pleaded with me to go with her. I insisted that I needed to stay and be with my fellow volunteers.

I don't know what I would have done without her. She was able to leave me enough money to stay in Ghana until the group arrived, which became my lifeline. I only brought my backpack containing a bathing suit, 2 *pagnes,* and two t-shirts plus what I was wearing, another *pagne* that I wore tied at my waist and a t-shirt.

When I met up with my friend Blair who had sent me an e-mail from Benin where she was traveling. We met up and together we explored Elmina's fishing village which is very quaint, unlike anything in the Ivory Coast where the people don't like to fish. They buy their fish from Ghana which is located on the same water as they are. I guess they would rather work in the fields with their machetes. We watched the big handsome men working and singing their "heave ho" kind of songs and enjoyed seeing them bring in their catch of the day.

Driving down the street, you see places that are called, "Dear Jesus and Co." or "Holy Lord Enterprises" and the like. The missionaries have done their work in Ghana, that is for sure. There was even a brass band marching up the street where everyone was wearing white t-shirts and singing and waving banners about Jesus Christ and it wasn't Easter!

Cape Coast Castle is a "slave castle" and fort built by the Portuguese where they traded gold and people between 1526 and 1867. We walked through the important tourist attraction to view the last experience that the men and women had in their own country before their final departure at the "door of no return". There was not a dry eye in sight when we saw how many people were crammed into the different small spaces where they were detained, and how they kept the more attractive women for the Captain. It was a monument of acknowledgement, and to preserve the deeply painful past of slavery, and the sufferings endured by these people. The fort raises awareness about the history of slavery and how it impacted society. Nobody could talk while we filed off the ship completely wrung by the utter cruelty inflicted on those other human beings.

We checked our e-mails at a local internet café to find some hopeful news. Blair and I were told by the Peace Corps to go to the sister hotel of the fancy place where Janet and I stayed and check in and eat all of our meals there. She was young and followed a very healthy regime and was a good example for me. It was the largest hotel, more like a resort, that could accommodate all of the volunteers and staff from the

110

Côte d'Ivoire. The staff did certainly take care of us. No more eating grilled plantains and peanuts on the street for us trying to economize.

When we arrived at the hotel in Accra, we were astonished to find Charles Taylor from Liberia decorated in full military regalia leaving the front door along with other dignitaries. He had a commanding and charismatic presence with an imposing stature. He was later convicted for crimes against humanity, now serving 50 years in prison. There was a meeting taking place where many of the representatives from different West African countries were seen filing out the door behind him. The heavyweights were said to be strategizing about the political unrest in the Ivory Coast.

"It is completely against Peace Corps policy to hold any money in your house." The rules kept running in my mind about my hidden *agouti* and the micro-financing money. I began to wonder who was going to find that money... and all those empty wine bottles. The Peace Corps said that they would go to our sites and pack up the things that we wanted. I really didn't expect them to find the money because I imagined that everyone had already pilfered through all of my belongings, certainly not waiting for a list of instructions delivered by Peace Corps. Years later it was recounted to me that my friend Carine took charge right away and had first pick no matter what my wishes happened to be. I was very fortunate to be the recipient of some beautiful blue and yellow "made in Provence" kitchenware, complete with matching utensils, dishes and glasses, and also a small refrigerator from a kind volunteer, Mark, who had already finished his service and donated them to me. The items were the envy of the women who saw them, and how I enjoyed using them!

My head was abuzz. What about the little girls who used to come over every morning and sweep the front of my house for cookies or some coins? And little Willie and his friends? What about all the clubs I started in the schools in all those villages... and I would just disappear?

The volunteers were all asking themselves and each other the same things, "Would we ever see our friends again in the villages where we lived? Would we ever return? Would all the volunteers make it to Ghana unharmed?"

The Peace Corps provided psychological counseling for those who wanted it. I thought, why not. It was helpful to spill out my emotions to a professional, and was glad I did. He told me I could let it out with a primal scream because I had so much angst... and that felt really good.

After a military evacuation using C160 and C130 planes and Cougar helicopters for some volunteers who were in real danger up north, we waited breathlessly for over a week for the last volunteer, Alex, to join us. We all cried tears of joy at the sight of her when she walked into our meeting room because, finally, we were all safe, present, and accounted for. The volunteers who arrived late were all exhausted and told many stories. One that made us laugh was that the rebels wore stolen clothing from the Ivorian police while sporting their own jelly shoes. And the not so funny...they said that there were blockades set up all over with big military AK 47's pointing at them, and were trapped in their villages with food supplies dwindling and gunfire right outside their doors.

There were rebels and roaming gangs that were said to have burned people alive who were supporting the government during an exodus of thousands of people carrying cooking pots and bundles of clothes from the country's second largest city, Bouake. The rebels attempted to seize power in a coup plotted by Guei, who was killed by the loyalist forces. Most of the fighting was there, and in Korhogo and Abidjan with about 80 dead and many injured.

"Côte d'Ivoire entered the hearts of the volunteers in ways we could never have imagined," a friend wrote to me during the aftermath. The thought of never returning was a gut punch when we all heard the news that Washington, on that October 3rd day in 2002, declared that they decided to indefinitely suspend Peace Corps, Ivory Coast.

The volunteers were offered the choice of going home with a signed letter from the President or receiving a reassignment. I had 5 more months before the end of my two-year, three-month commitment and chose to get reassigned. I would go wherever I was wanted and needed and let them know without hesitation.

When I heard, "It's Kenya for Patricia Mertz!" the news brought tears. I thought it was an interception from my mother because of my promise to her when I knew she had to be thinking of Kenya. She spoke fondly of their people, the Masai Mara tribe and the wildlife. I had not only kept a promise to my mother to go to Africa but now, I was invited to work in Kenya, a place she and my father both loved.

Kenya

The new training was near the very lush Lake Naivasha, where light pink flamingos go to breed and where millions of dollars of cut flowers are exported. Bird watchers come from all over the world and take photos of the 400 different species in the birder's paradise. It was indeed a lush garden located far from the tropical red clay earth where I lived in Braffouéby.

Halfway through the group of Kenya volunteers' training, together with 3 other volunteers from the Côte d'Ivoire, we arrived in Naivasha. The others didn't know or seem to understand that leaving our previous posts was a traumatic experience for us, and that we carried a lot of emotional baggage. We agreed that it wasn't particularly easy to get to know the new people, most likely because we were missing our old friends. I had a big case of the blues.

During the training, a large family welcomed me to their farm situated down a dirt road in a thick forest. It reminded me of what the

Walton's stone farmhouse was possibly like. It had four couches covered in crocheted pink and white blankets and three armchairs that had little coffee tables in front of them where we all ate our strange but delicious cabbage dinners.

They grew and sold their fruit and raised chickens, sheep, and goats. Every morning they would get up at sunrise to bring their goods to the market to earn their living. I would rise after they left in the morning to find my warmed-up bucket of water for my bucket bath that I would take outside. And then find my way to training, often becoming disoriented, exasperated, and late for class. One corner of a dirt road lined with dense tree canopies looked like the next. At least the climate was more forgiving, not quite so hot and the roads were not so treacherous.

Among the new group of volunteers, there was a most charming and respected couple that had spent their retirement years doing Peace Corps volunteer service all over the world after distinguished careers as professors at Stanford University, Marsha and John. Kenya was their fifth assignment, and John was turning 80 years old! They both had luminous, resting smile faces, the likes of which I had never seen. The volunteers planned to perform a skit to honor him at the celebration. There were songs, dances, and another volunteer played his guitar. I offered to do a Marilyn Monroe happy birthday routine vaguely reminiscent of how she sang for JFK. The markets sold Smirnoff vodka in little packets in Kenya grocery stores that looked like the soy sauce packets you get in a Chinese take-out that we soon came to call "soy sauce" as code. I drank a couple of "soy sauces" to get myself in the Marilyn frame of mind, swiped on some red lipstick, found a tight sweater with lots of padding in my brassiere, and then sang a very low-key exaggerated version of the "Happy Birthday" song, since I can hardly carry a tune anyway. Working together on our program for John broke the ice. We all had many laughs, and I was happy to get to know, love, and appreciate the multitude of bright, talented, funny, and creative people in our Peace Corps Kenya group.

After training, I was assigned to Gatunguru, a small town with a large school for boys up high in the tea plantations near Thika. During the day, everything stops for their English-style tea ritual that is served with fresh non-homogenized milk. Their main food was beans. I thought I had problems in the Ivory Coast with food, but with my new diet of beans and milk, not that the cabbage dinners at the farm were kind to my digestive tract, I suffered from cramping beyond my imagination. They had assigned a family to prepare my meals until I offered to take charge of my food after realizing that my diet had to change. They were bewildered about what to prepare for me, so was I, but I convinced them that I could cook my own food, craving my independence.

I almost burned the place down when I turned on the propane tank for the stove. It exploded with a crash boom in my face leaving me badly burned after I lit a match. The fire also damaged most of the wall. The neighbors came running in to save me and to assess the damage while shaking their heads in horror. I needed to find a happy solution to my food issues, so I asked them to please make me some rice and add any sauce with anything on it other than beans. There was goat and kale on a plate for me the next meal. I was dreaming of peanut butter.

Electricity was on for three hours in the evening from a generator that sounded like a lawn moor and a leaf blower on full blast up your arse. I had electricity during a block of time, so, I couldn't complain. The view was extraordinary over the hills but unfortunately, they blocked the view with an outhouse and a shower. Sometimes I brought a wooden chair outside on the neighbor's side to sit for a moment to appreciate the vast beauty and tranquility.

There was an indoor toilet that was a porcelain hole in the floor with a chain that flushed it. When Mike and Matt visited, Mike wore his very long scarf wrapped around his head to prevent any foul smells from entering his pampered nostrils.

After living in West Africa, with temperatures of 95 degrees and above, I was very cold living up in the hills at 65-70 degrees. It was rainy with a whole lot of mud everywhere. Since I did not have the right clothing or any of my belongings, for that matter, I figured out how to get to Nairobi from my new site. There was an outdoor market near the bus station where I found a suitable wardrobe by picking through the mountains of recycled clothes paid for by the Peace Corps stipend and leftover Janet money. There were some good quality used t-shirts and skirts available, mostly sent from Great Britain and the US, before China flooded the markets with their cheap knockoffs. A real find was an authentic t-shirt from a random rock concert or a throwaway from a manufacturer who had spelled something wrong, and some warm sweaters too. I bought a sweatshirt that said, "Just use it", that I imagined was referring to a condom.

Clothes were easy to find, but my main stress was the money that I had hidden for our micro financing project because I knew that I let the women down. I could live with losing the agouti money because the donors, son Mike and brother Pete would understand the circumstances. N'Guesson would be disappointed but he, nevertheless, learned a new skill of *agouti* farming but he had no money to raise the animals.

N'Guesson, my trustworthy friend from Braffouéby, and I were steadfast in trying to convince a group of women to believe in saving a portion of their money they earned from selling at the market, so they could become eligible for a loan for their businesses. It was a slow process and a hard sell, but finally, we won over a strong female group in Sikensi, and I was, unfortunately, the bank for them. Some women were afraid their spouses would find out and be angry that they didn't give all their proceeds from their sales in the market to them. Several attempts were made to deliver the money to the women after I left, but the money never made it to N'Guesson. Finally, way too many years later, they did, in fact, receive their money, hand delivered by me.

The pope had just come out with an edict that people should practice chastity and not to promote condom use when I arrived. What? Tell that to a 17 year old. My job was to help prevent HIV/AIDS and besides abstinence, condoms were the only way.

I agreed to show a film with one of the health workers to a boy's class, without ever viewing the film first. It was produced by a Christian group that was vehemently against condoms and it's message was to promote abstinence. I had to keep my mouth shut during the showing of it, but I escorted the woman out after it finished, and immediately gave the students the message that if you decide that you are going to have sex, please protect yourself and your partner with a condom.

The Kikuyu tribe is in the majority in Kenya, the most ambitious tribe, and usually, they make the most money farming sheep and cattle. A cab driver who was not Kikuyu told me that the Kikuyu did not always care for their young people, other than their own children because they did not want to spend any money on anyone other than their own. I remembered how the Abidgis from Braffouéby absorbed orphaned children into their own homes no matter how poor they were or even if they were not related.

Christmas Vacation

Michael and Matthew were coming to visit me in Gatunguru for Christmas. I had been counting the days to see them since I left but never knew when they would decide to make the trip. The timing wasn't great because there was an election coming up on December 27th. During the previous election, violence had erupted, which resulted in riots and death. The edict from the Country Director was in stone, "Volunteers were to stay at their sites over Christmas". I made a special plea to receive permission to go on safari with my children with the agreement, "under no circumstances" were we to visit Mombasa on the Indian Ocean.

117

"How can we be that close to the Indian Ocean and not visit it?" Michael reasoned.

"Mom, it's the Indian Ocean! I must see every one of the oceans," Matthew argued.

Wouldn't you know it, Mike and Matt were hell-bent on going to Mombasa, and they hammered away at me. My two sons together know how to wear me down and I ultimately acquiesced.

We checked into the Norfolk Hotel in Nairobi that is now owned by the Fairmont. It is a classic beloved hotel established in 1904 with old-world charm of historic proportions. The bar itself was an elegant throwback to another era. I wanted to linger there and not be in a hurry to jump into the next event.

A thoughtful Peace Corps friend, Ting, arranged a "Welcome to Nairobi Party" for my sons at an Ethiopian restaurant in a party room the evening they arrived. We ate their spongey bread, injera, with all the warm, delicious stews and meats at a big, long table filled with my new gregarious twenty-something friends. Mary K Blige belting out "Family Affair" on the jukebox prompted dancing after dinner while we drank quantities of our new favorite beer, Tusker. It was a perfect "karibu" welcome and send-off before traveling back to my site with my sons to visit Gatunguru.

I carefully arranged to have a recommended driver who knew his way around take us to my new home. We packed up his car and took off for the hills! I was so happy to have my sons next to me in Kenya, as I had never before been separated from them for so long.

When we were leaving the intensity of bustling, frenetic, crowded Nairobi, we were stopped in traffic when a young, sweet, but scruffy-looking child came up to the car asking for money. Mike and Matt reached in their pockets and gave him some shillings, but before we drove away from the scene, the older kids sprang out from behind the cars and grabbed the child's cash.

Mike quipped, "That's the law of the streets, mom."

The AIDS epidemic hit Kenya dramatically during that time when many children were living on the street. There were gangs of them, many AIDS orphans, who I knew, engaged in petty thievery sometimes walking around Nairobi and smaller towns. One day in Thika, which was the largest town near me, a young child ran by and grabbed the sunglasses right off my face. Many of the young street kids were sniffing glue, dirty, homeless, and desperate. The smell of glue was overpowering as you walk down the streets in Nairobi or Thika. They sniffed the glue because it eliminated the pain of hunger.

Without the assistance of the local nuns, many of the street children would not have had a meal or at least some daily bread and tea and, I am quite sure, a few good moral lessons.

My sons and I were finally on the busy highway headed to Gatunguru, about 35 miles north of Nairobi, which led to the last leg, a lonely road that approached the village that winds and climbs up a hill. It is void of any traffic. As I was pointing out the tea pickers with their baskets strapped to their backs over on the hillside, a gang of youths carrying machetes, sticks and rocks jumped in front of the car out of nowhere and formed a blockade. Our driver was visibly alarmed shaking with fear and came to a complete stop. His reaction did not have a calming effect on my sons, to say the least. Matt and Mike both ordered the driver to turn around.

"Get out of here …fast." They demanded in loud voices. "Mom, we are not going up there!" "Driver, turn around!"

I was undaunted. There was not going to be an incident, not on my watch. Nobody was going to disrupt our plans. I maintained my composure.

In the next minute or so, I looked over at the driver's window while the hoodlums surrounded the car, when out of the blue, Nixon appeared, the 6'6 headmaster of the school where I worked. He had the most radiant smile I ever saw. His head was larger than life as the driver rolled down the window. All he said was "Karibu," welcome in Kiswahili. He then stood straight up and began walking towards the youths. The whole "gang of cutthroats" scattered everywhere, and peace was immediately restored. We all took a breath.

Nixon calmly closed off the subject, "No big deal because nothing happened."

We never spoke of the incident again. But later in the day, when Mike, Matt and I walked over to the village shops greeting everyone with "jambo" along the way, my sons left me outside in front of the tailor and, after a few minutes, reappeared with a 3' machete for me to keep "for protection."

Since we only had a couple of days together in Gatunguru, I wanted Mike and Matt to have maximum exposure to the culture and, of course, show them off to my new community. I decided to take them to church on Sunday.

When we arrived, one of the ushers escorted us up to the very first pew down in the front. The students were divided into three groups of girls and three groups of boys according to their ages, and each choral group was to perform their chosen hymn at the altar before the congregation, starting with the youngest girls first. At about the end of the boy's intermediate group, not even halfway through, Mike reached out to hold my hand, which I thought was sweet, and looked over at him lovingly, until he started squeezing it very hard until it was no longer sweet and tender. He wanted the service to be over. I looked at him, still smiling lovingly, and spoke, trying not to move my lips because I knew we were on display, "Relax". Some things never change, I thought, as I flashed back to a memory of my impatient son in church at age two yelling out during the mass in the middle of the consecration, "All done, church, all done." We made it through the singing performances and the collection followed after.

It was traditional that if somebody had little money for an offering, that person brought in something to donate to the priest, who auctioned it off to the highest bidder. A man brought up a live chicken to the front of the church as his gift. Mike and Matt immediately sat up straight and became fully alert as the bidding began. Everyone soon realized that, eventually, the two of them were bidding against each other and had just set a record for most shillings ever spent on an auction, I was told. Matthew outbid Mike. Matt proudly walked up to make his donation and claim his prize chicken. I think he had seen too many cartoons where you hold a rubber chicken by the feet upside down, which is what he did. The poor chicken started squawking loudly, feathers flying and was furiously wriggling to try and escape. Mike and I looked at each other. We stood up and accompanied Matthew, the chicken, and a parishioner, who came to the aid of the chicken, and we all walked down the middle aisle and out the front door, much to the relief of the congregation and to the relief of my sons.

After church, before we left for our Christmas holiday, I accepted an invitation for tea from a family who had always been very kind to me. Mike and Matt passed on eating any of their food or fruit, were fidgeting and awkwardly drinking the tea in their designated chairs. I don't know if they were ever at an event where nobody had much to say other than minimal polite conversation.

The father mentioned a chicken coop located in their backyard. Upon hearing the news, my sons asked permission to go out and see it, looking for an excuse to leave the tea party, I was sure. We accompanied them around the back when Matthew broke away from us and vaulted across the fence inside of the coop flapping his arms, squatting, and hopping to his version of a chicken dance. He met the terrified squawking chickens who could not escape from him fast enough. There was pandemonium.

I was incredulous and dashed over to order him to remove himself from the coop immediately. Mike was beside himself with laughter and could hardly regain his composure. We thanked our hosts whole-heartedly for their kind invitation while I ushered them both as quickly as possible out the door. Matthew's prize church chicken was donated to our tea party hosts to cook and enjoy for their Christmas holiday meal.

We hit the road after many farewells, and soon we were on our way to Mombasa, hopefully, to find a lovely hotel to please my discriminating sons. Admittedly, the places I chose did not match the advertised descriptions. Perhaps the hotels were grand twenty-five years ago, but unfortunately, the passing of time was unkind to them. I had prepaid the rooms and knew I had a fight ahead of me to obtain refunds. I could have cared less at the time because it was glorious to be with them.

We were in Mombasa for the results of the election, which surprised us with absolutely the most joyful, exuberant, and emotional demon-stration of love and hope for the future that ever happened for a winning candidate, Mwai Kibaki. People went wild with jubilation, yelling and waving tree branches, dancing on the cars and in the streets, with music and cheering that exploded into the late night.

My boys asked, "What is the worst thing that could ever happen to you, Mom, if it was discovered that we did go to Mombasa?"

"I would be asked to leave the Peace Corps," I responded

"What," Mike flippantly said, "you would get kicked out?"

My sons didn't understand how great of an honor it was for me to be a part of something as big as the Peace Corps. I learned from highly skilled, interesting, and dedicated people from Kenya and the Ivory Coast about the culture and traditions and about their specific circum-stances in ways that I could never read about in a book. They inspired me to give my best and the bonus was that I was surrounded by talented volunteers who were there to have fun, find adventure and do good.

They teased me like little bratty boys when they watched me devour my food at a restaurant and then reminded me that there would be more food coming at the next meal. Admittedly, I was very hungry and found myself eating off their plates as well as mine. They pranked me at the restaurant when I was trying to find my way back from a trip to the Ladies' Room. They saw me walk around past our table instead of waving or calling my name. It wasn't very funny, and I told them that they were impolite. I didn't know at the time, and neither did they, that I had a severe case of cataracts. I knew I could hardly see anything, but I thought that maybe my contact lenses were blurry and old, and I am extremely myopic. It was still glorious to be with them.

The Maasai Mara tribe in the Savannah grasslands was worth the hype and more. The Maasai people, in their fanciful tartan plaid dress, are every bit as hospitable and energetic as is said of them. I knew why my mother had fallen in love with the tribe and the raw beauty of nature. On safari, we hired a jeep with a guide and were fortunate to see a lion with its prey, wildebeests, herds of zebras, a rhino, a cheetah on the prowl, and many elegant giraffes.

Figure 22 Matthew and Michael standing with me on the Tanzania/Kenyan border

When Mike and Matt left for the airport, I languished for a while, while they were off to meet their friends in Europe for the new year celebration. When they were younger, their vacations were with my

123

whole family in Florida, but when it was just the three of us, after my divorce, we would usually find our own fun by going to state parks, hiking along the trails, and staying in rustic cabins in the wilderness. Sometimes on the road trip, I would pray for a good song so I could turn up the volume on the radio and drown out their bickering in the back seat of the car and all sing along. Our trip to Africa was indelible.

Besides my stomach, I had a really difficult time with my eyes in Kenya. If somebody changed their shirt, it was a strain to know who they were because I could not make out distinctions in people's faces. I thought there was something wrong with my brain and continued to clean my contacts until I received the diagnosis. They called me in for a health check-up, only to find out that I needed surgery immediately. The Peace Corps had a doctor in Nairobi who they suggested would perform the cataract surgery, but since I was already so nearsighted, I realized the surgery would be extra tricky. I did not want to chance having anyone but an American doctor work on my eyes.

The next day I was medically evacuated to DC and stayed 40 days in Georgetown to have both eyes done. My cousin Chas lived nearby and treated me to beautiful dinners and champagne in chic restaurants and in his lavish home. What a luxurious place to come home to after Africa, both in a Georgetown hotel and being spoiled at my cousin's!

Historically, it was a turbulent time in America. Congress had granted President Bush authority to declare war on Iraq. I marched for peace and held lit candles just like in the 60's at a large demonstration held at the Washington Monument where Joan Baez sang her crystal-clear ballads.

The actual day that I was ticketed to return to Kenya after I was released from the doctor's care was on the actual day the US was to start bombing Iraq. I was fraught with uncertainty. With only 3 weeks left of my service, I decided not to return to Gatunguru. Leaving both countries abruptly, Ivory Coast and Kenya, was deeply unsettling.

Back Home

Back home, Chicago felt strange, even if we were counseled about the adjustment we would face. I stayed with my sister Janet in Chicago because I had sold my condo while I was gone, and she was generous to open her doors to me.

Janet likes to tell the story about my first trip to the Jewel Food Store when she happened to be there at the same time that I was shopping. I was reminded of the myriad of mind-blowing choices available to us in our grocery stores. As I was being dazzled by the well-stocked shelves and colorful, eye-popping displays, I noticed a hanging sign on a shopping cart that read, "$1 for everything in the basket." I believed I had just happened upon the most outrageous cut-rate bargains ever. The cart was filled with every food and bottle of wine that I liked, from the bread to the coffee to the cheese and my favorite crackers, even peanut butter. I started eagerly emptying the contents of the $1 cart into my own empty cart. When I looked up, I saw my sister standing in front of me, laughing out loud, asking me what I was doing. I was delighted to share my discovery.

"Patsy," she said, "Look, that sign is on everyone in the store's grocery cart."

Evidently, to my surprise, there was one cart filled with broken boxes of food and such in the back of the store where one finds the dollar deals. Following my embarrassment, I trailed along with Janet to the check-out area. I looked at the clerk and then at Janet to see if there was a reaction when they saw the price of the coffee. I was shocked to see how expensive it was and asked the check-out person if she would please give us a better price. Janet promptly whisked me out of there.

I had developed a hypersensitivity to our prosperity and abundance and how everything they had in Africa did not come easy. Sometimes I would talk to strangers about the poverty and malnutrition that exists in the places where I was located and felt hopeless. I had a one-way conversation with a sales clerk in a gift shop about what I had witnessed and then burst out crying in front of her. I can still see her face turning from empathy to pity to "That woman is crazy."

Soon after, my family and I went on a beach vacation to Anna Maria Island, FL. During the night before my pre-planned side trip to visit friends in Fort Lauderdale, I had malaria spikes with chills and hot sweats. The spell only lasted a minute or so, and the Peace Corps doctors warned us that it was normal after taking the prescribed malaria prophylactic for over two years.

In the past, I would hop on a plane or drive a car across the state to see my friends, but I took a bus since I was still in an African state of mind. My dear old friends picked me up at the station and by the time we all sat down in their lovely well appointed living room with a chilled glass of wine, I struggled to feel relaxed and would not surrender to whatever was happening inside of my body.

Mike, my friend, said, "Patsy, you haven't touched your drink!" which was very much out of character for me.

The same sensations as the night before began to overcome me, but I inherently knew the "spikes" wouldn't go away this time. I began shaking and shivering and couldn't stop even with the ton of blankets Lois placed on me. My temperature shot up. I was burning hot. They took me to Broward Medical Center after Mike called his doctor friend. I knew it was malaria. The medical team thought it was conta- gious and dressed up in suits and hoods. I told them I didn't bring the mosquitos with me, but they didn't think that was funny. I knew they had to take every precaution when they learned I was coming from East and West Africa and immediately, the staff placed me in isolation. That wasn't the last time that I was hospitalized after a trip back from the Ivory Coast, there were many more trips to emergency rooms and hospital beds, but the only other time for malaria.

Broward is a teaching hospital and I think they kept me there for four extra days because the medical students let me know that they hadn't ever seen a malaria case. I was relieved to learn that they had the strongest, most current medicine available for the cure.

I recuperated at the home of my parents' loving friends in Vero Beach, who treated me like royalty. Mary and Dick had stacks of brand-new books at my bedside, a dish of chocolates, fresh water, flowers, delicious meals served on fine china on a tray, plus a big fluffy bed and the sheets were divine. I have loved those two people my whole life and I used to follow them around whenever they came over to our family house as a child. It took me a while to get my strength back to travel home, not that I malingered for too long, maybe a little, and they were so gracious.

As I was resting comfortably in my cushy environment, I could not stop thinking about how many people get malaria in the hot and steamy village with no medical care and how they continue to look after their children and perform their back-breaking chores. The thoughts weighed heavy. If I was going to get malaria, I could not have been more fortunate than to get it back home in the USA, chez Sweeney, in a fine hospital and to recover chez Schaub.

Italy

One long hot day back in the Ivory Coast, after a full day racing between schools and working with the young people, I was worn out from my stomach aches and the endless walking in the oppressive heat. What I needed for my mental health was to look forward to something extraordinary after my service.

"I am going to Italy!" I said to myself in a lightbulb moment, not knowing how I was going to make it happen.

My spirits immediately brightened upon a visit to the Peace Corps office computer the moment I discovered a three-month program in

Rome to get certified to teach English. My next step was setting up the route to get there. Since I would have the whole summer to be home and see everyone, in the Fall, I planned to take off to the Roman school to learn to teach English as a second language, get certified, and then hopefully, find a job teaching English somewhere in Italy.

The English teaching course in Rome ended right before Christmas. I was grateful that the nuns had given me one good thing, a strong grammar foundation. I assiduously sent out over 200 online and 100 written resumes with letters to every school I could find who might be looking for an ESL teacher. I received only one response out of all of them from St. Peter's English Language School in Napoli. My adventurous 23-year-old roommate, Renee, who attended classes with me in Rome, asked if she could go with me on the train trip down south for my job interview.

During my interview meeting with the distinguished school Director, a true English gentleman the likes of whom I had never met, asked me one very direct question, "Why St. Peter's?" I desperately wanted this job because I did not have a plan B.

I did not tell him that St. Peter's was the only school that responded to my resumes. I did tell him the true story, "When I sealed the envelope that I sent to you, I kissed it and said a little prayer hoping for an interview because my brother's and my two Nephews' names are Peter."

I immediately dissolved in tears and fumbled for a kleenex without success and tore off a corner of a white bag that was filled with St Francis medals I had just bought in Assisi. He noticed my distress and plucked his light-colored silk handkerchief out of the front pocket of his perfectly tailored jacket and handed it to me, swiveled his chair around so that his back was facing me while I wiped my tears and regained my composure. I felt so embarrassed that I wanted to cry but I was already doing that.

When he turned his seat around to face me again, he offered me the job and gave me a full schedule. I had no idea that it was the norm that a new teacher would be required to give a demonstration as part of the interview and would usually have a schedule where you only start teaching about four hours a week. He informed me that I would have a full forty-hour schedule after a two week probation period. I held back a giant "whoopee" inside and lit up in gratitude and glee.

As I glided down the grand winding staircase joyfully holding onto the thick brass railing of the ornate school building with its Italianate architecture situated on the elegant boulevard along the Mediterranean Sea, my friend Renee was waiting for me outside the giant glass door and ready to celebrate my good news. The streets were old and convoluted, so that I could never find my way around Naples unless I was following "the Captain," as my sons later nicknamed Renee. She said that she had family living in a town nearby and that she wanted to live and work in Napoli too.

"I have a roommate and a job!" I declared.

We walked around the corner and stumbled upon an American elementary school, wandered in, she interviewed, and was instantly hired. Subsequently, we had three great reasons to celebrate.

Renee was going home for Christmas and I decided that in lieu of me going home after my courses were completed, I decided to meet my friend Skip in Paris, who had previously invited me to Bora Bora. I enjoyed his "joie de vivre" and his love of all things French. Being such old friends, I never had to explain much. He bought me a beautiful room in an elegant hotel in Montmartre and he was staying in the Place de Voges at a friend's home.

He asked me if I would pick up some tickets for us to see the "Tango" live production at the Théâtre Champs- Elysée on the very chic Avenue Montaigne in the 8th arrondissement.

"Of course," I said, "I would be delighted to."

While I was passing by the Louis Vuitton store, I noticed that there was a long line of people standing outside their door, which I found to be rather odd. Two Asian girls approached me to relay their sob story about how the store refused to sell them anything. The emotionally distressed young women could not understand the reason why they were refused entry and begged me for help. Much later, I discovered that many people were selling luxury goods to the profitable Asian black markets, but I was unaware of that fact at the time. Hence, I dismissed the two women saying, "I am sorry, but I really am in a bit of a hurry!"

They pleaded with me until they convinced me that the store was discriminating against them. They ultimately hit my sympathetic and righteous for justice nerve with their tearful pleas. I broke down and said I would stand in line and buy them whatever they wanted. They handed me a folded pack of euros that felt thick enough so that I didn't even bother counting it and did not want to call any attention to the money. One of the women described in detail the wallets I was requested to purchase. We agreed to meet at the same exact place where they stopped me.

As I was standing in the line, a young, polished, and très chic gentleman approached me to ask if I intended to buy the items for myself. He continued in English in a low voice, "You are not to buy for anyone except for yourself."

I was indignant and lied, "But of course, I am shopping for myself."

As I was getting closer to the front of the line, a stylish young woman with freshly applied red lipstick asked me the same question, also in English.

I then repeated without hesitation the same answer, "Mais, oui," I said, trying to sound French, "C'est pour moi-même."

The mademoiselle was very serious and went on to stress the extreme importance of my being truthful. My heart was beginning to pound, and my face was flushed as I was now nearing the entrance of the store.

Another gorgeous model-type woman walked over towards me to accompany me inside after I arrived at the front of the line. She informed me in her very direct, most polite manner that there were police hiding outside behind the bushes and that I would be arrested if it was discovered that I bought anything in the store for another person.

This is all too much, I thought. My heart was racing, and my face was now turning beet red and pulsating.

By this time, I was very angry at myself for getting into the situation. She slowly escorted me up to the sparkling glass case inside with all the outrageously expensive L/V merchandise meticulously arranged.

Another model-type person approached me from behind the counter. I looked the salesperson in the eye before his sales pitch and said, "You know, I believe that I have changed my mind," and then I turned around and walked out the door to find my cohorts in crime and give them the unfortunate news and return the big wad of money.

They were not there! I walked up and down the block and saw no police and not even one Asian woman anywhere. I stopped to survey the scene but was losing patience. I was panicking and felt guilty about my lies and just wanted to end my predicament and get the hell out of there.

Not knowing where else to turn, I noticed an entrance to a metro station nearby. I instantly descended the staircase and boarded the first train that appeared. I attempted to change my appearance by digging out my oversized Italian designer sunglasses from my bag, untied my neck scarf to tie on my head, and then opened my purse to surreptitiously count the money in an empty seat. I felt like I was in a movie. My wad of euros was worth over $1500.

"Oh my God," I gasped. All that money and I still had to go back to the neighborhood to buy the theatre tickets!

I boarded another train going in the reverse direction, returned to the original Metro station, walked up the stairs at Avenue Montaigne and scanned the scene again for the women and the police.

They disappeared, no doubt about it.

The line had shrunk to only three people.

What do I do? I pondered and then spotted the 5-star Plaza Athénée Hotel nearby. Aha! What a lovely place to think this whole thing through.

I entered the elegant holiday-decorated lobby with my load of cash, looked around and was escorted to an inviting table near the shining silver and gold Christmas tree. While inhaling the calm and luxurious ambiance, I skimmed through the gold-threaded menu and promptly ordered shrimp and champagne from the formally clad waiter.

What the hell. I thought.

I called my friend, Skip, and told him about the unlikely chain of events, and then my phone went dead before he could reply. It was complicated in those early days of European cell phones to find an establishment that sold usage units for mobile phones.

I bravely walked past the Louis Vuitton store again after my little respite, still wearing my disguise. I decided to hand over the money if I spotted them minus the bill at the hotel. Still no sight of them. I headed towards the ticket booth and bought the two tickets for the production and stopped along the avenue on a few more errands, feeling flush from my windfall.

Skip was at the designated restaurant waiting for me for 45 minutes. I had the theatre tickets and a phone that worked. I was wearing a shiny new pair of shoes I spotted in a window, and I had a lot more money in my purse, thanks to the Asians. Skip thought I was captured and taken hostage by the Asian mafia because I didn't call him back. He was angry and not amused because he believed "the mob had indeed found me, chopped me up, and stuffed me somewhere," he ranted on and on, and he wouldn't let me buy dinner.

Napoli

Renee's relatives lived an hour's train ride away from Naples in Capriati, a most inviting little village nestled in the mountains. Her gregarious family met us when we arrived at the station with warm embraces and kisses three times on alternate cheeks. Upon every visit to their village, her great uncle would say to me, "Oh, Patrizia, your Italian is getting worse instead of better," and we would all have a hearty laugh. Their traditional Sunday dinners with the extended family were monumental and lasted for hours with copious delicious courses of their favorite family recipes accompanied by the local wines. One brother had a bread factory, another canned the tomatoes, a sister was a doctor, another was a lawyer, and another was in politics and, of course, they knew everyone in town. We feasted like the Romans until the evening when Carmine would top off the meal with a heady licorice-tasting *digestivo* to soothe the stomach. The family celebrated either someone of their own, a birthday or anniversary, some obscure saint's feast day that the Italians seemed to have every other day, or simply the fact that it was Sunday dinner and everyone was together.

During May, we were invited to hike in a procession up a local hill together with the villagers to honor the Virgin Mother, where there was an altar and statue covered with bountiful Spring flowers. It was an opportunity to play games, listen to music, meet their friends, speak Italian and for us all to feast and drink wine in Mary's honor until sundown.

The people I met in Napoli were warm and open to me, but I was a nine-time target for the underground petty thieves. The Italian police had recently taken away their black-market sales of cigarettes, so at least nine of those little punks found me as a target to help supplement their incomes. I was advised by another teacher to dye my blonde hair black or brown so as not to stand out.

One evening at nightfall, I was with my friends, Jill and Alice, who both urged me to go with them to their favorite pizza place. Since it was dusk and located down a narrow dark street, I argued that there would be no way in hell that I would walk there.

They maintained, "No, no, you will be safely walking in the middle, and we will be holding on to you on both sides and you will be fine."

I agreed because I had heard many times that the pizza at *Di Matteo* was "delizioso," and besides, the two of them had never been robbed, and maybe they were good luck. We began our stroll down the ancient, cobbled street and before I knew it, a kid on a motorbike swooped over in front of me and grabbed the strap of my purse off my shoulder while I hung on desperately to it and to the arms of my friends. He mistakenly thought I would let go. He failed to get my bag, but the incident was infuriating, and I was left with a sore arm and shoulder and thoroughly disillusioned.

The worst hit on me was when we arrived back in Naples after our Christmas holiday. Renee and I were staying at a hotel near the train station in the Piazza Garibaldi that turned out to be a flop house filled with every other degenerate in the city, including the *signorinas* of the night who we would pass on the stairway or in the lobby.

The two of us ventured across town to search for our new apartment that I found in the local paper in a busy neighborhood with transport nearby. We had already viewed it once and were very anxious to make our final arrangements. I was carrying our first month's rent plus the deposit. Immediately upon arriving, the owners declared that they had changed their minds for some sketchy reason and decided not to rent the apartment to us after all. They saw where I had placed our money and the required passport, which was in a fabric wallet around my neck. They even so much as offered to give me one of their own money pouches and the information on where to stand to find a bus back to our hotel.

"Isn't that so very nice?" Renee heard me murmur sarcastically. We were not happy, now faced again with the challenging task of starting over to find a suitable place for us to live. Many places simply did not take foreigners.

Just before boarding the bus, I was robbed outside of their building by two men and a woman, and I was left with no money, no debit card, and no passport on top of not having an apartment. Those three were pros. We had come this far and I was not giving up yet.

When I dialed each of my sons for help, neither one answered their phones. Probably still sleeping, I thought. My brother Peter was next on the list. He didn't hesitate to leave his football game and venture out on that cold, snowy Sunday afternoon in Munster, Indiana, to wire me the money. The management at the hotel was kind enough to extend us credit and let us stay until I could obtain a new passport required to collect the funds, and time to find another place. Ranali, the Manager, became my first new best friend in Naples.

Renee and I landed a large apartment on the 7th floor of a building with a foundation built in 500 BC in the *citta vecchia*, the oldest section. I learned later from trusted sources that the neighborhood was not a desirable place for us to live, but there was nowhere available that we could afford that was more spacious and with more character and most importantly, who would accept us. It was grand and authentic. A coin was necessary to ride the antique elevator with a wire cage up to the seventh floor with ceilings so high that it was actually like living on the fourteenth floor. We exited into a courtyard surrounded by two other similarly built buildings where an old woman sat with a snarly face in the window across the way from morning till night. Every morning before work, I would yell, "Buon giorno," and wave to her. Never once did she respond.

One evening towards the end of the semester, my friend, Kelly, a schoolmate from Rome, was coming to stay with us and I arranged to meet her at a local neighborhood pizza place after school near where we lived. After our meal, just as it was getting dark, we headed down the narrow walkway around the corner under the clotheslines between the ancient buildings towards home. A rat pack of young boys appeared in front and behind us and grabbed my friend's suitcase and my backpack right in front of the courtyard's gate.

I began screaming and yelling like a banshee while hanging on tightly to my belongings, sadly in vain. People came out from every direction, all talking at the same time, mostly in their local language, Napolitano, not Italian.

One man stepped forward and said in Italian, "You have no business being here, lady."

At that moment, I looked over at an old traditional-looking woman in the crowd who spoke over them and said, "She lives over there. I know her." She was the weird cranky woman in the window!

The crowd backed off when the mysterious woman signaled us to follow her up to her apartment. She sat us both down in a kitchen chair. I was instructed to hold out both arms for her while she wrapped them with gauze like a mummy, not that plain gauze was a cure for sore arms, but it was her kind gesture that counted. My friend sat on a chair facing me in dazed bewilderment. After her wrap job, our queen of the courtyard ordered us to sit in her front room while she made some angry-sounding phone calls. We waited for over an hour without any updates. Meanwhile, Kelly became inconsolable over the loss of all of her belongings. I instinctively knew we had to obey the signora and urged her to please be patient and wait it out to see what would transpire.

I heard a loud ring and then lots of rumbling coming from the back stairs of the apartment before she answered the door. We stayed seated. Minutes later, the Signora walked into the room towards us, looking stern as ever and delivered my friend's suitcase with all the contents and my backpack minus my new Gucci sunglasses and, of course, the cash. She was the eyes and ears of the courtyard, and probably the leader of the pack.

She waved at me every morning thereafter, which even prompted a slight smile from her during my last days living there. There was a lot to love about fabulous Napoli, her lively, intense women, flirty men, the art and architecture, food, wine, artifacts, and majestic cathedrals, but being robbed nine times was never a good experience. When I moved out to return to Chicago the next week for the summer break, I gave the Signora my music system and a first-aid kit. Renee and I returned for another school year but in a neighborhood up the steep hill with beautiful scenery in Posillipo. My old pal from the Garibaldi brothel hotel held my luggage over the summer holiday until I returned.

I owe a lot to my dear friends in Italy, Renee, Alice, and Jill, who listened to me while I tossed around the idea of raising money to build a clinic in Africa. Although I felt the whole concept to be beyond anything that I could do, they were supportive listeners and exhibited no doubts about my abilities. I felt at ease with them revealing my dreams of bettering the lives of the women in the village with a maternity healthcare center. The old chief's heartbreaking story of the loss of his grandchild, and my own birth trauma with Matthew compounded by the stories of life and death from the many kind, hardworking women in the village, never went away.

Ivory Coast Mothers and Children

After almost two years in Italy, in late 2004, I came home for good. I found a new condo in an old, established neighborhood in the Ukrainian village of Chicago near my sons and my friends Margaret and Kevin, and not far from my sister, Janet. I became employed by Kevin and learned about the wireless telephone business for hospitals under his direction. "Smile and Dial" was the new credo. Going to lunch was my favorite part of the day, although I made some good money for myself and for the company with people I liked.

Africa was still hovering over me, and I still needed to talk about it. I told a story to my young niece, Lizzy, about the women in the village and how I was haunted by their suffering. She sat up, looked at me intensely with her big brown eyes and replied, not skipping a beat, "Aunt Patsy, what are you going to do about it?" That was the moment when for the first time, I wasn't rehearsing the idea with close friends. This time I said out loud to Lizzie that I was going to build a clinic there, and I meant it. I felt the earth shift. It was real. Earlier that same evening, I had told her about a singing contest in a Chicago bar where she could win $10,000 because she had a voice like an angel and that she could most likely win it all. In her next sentence, she told me she would enter the contest and if she won, she would donate all her winnings to build the clinic. I was flabbergasted. For six weeks, a group of my friends and family went to the bar up on the north side of Chicago on Thursday nights to cheer her on. She made it to the finals. The judges loved her, and the crowd loved her, but the winner depended on the votes of the people who were present at the bar during the final night of elimination. Sadly, we were not clever enough to bring in busloads of people to vote for her, as did the competition, and so she lost the number one prize, but she came in fourth place. Lizzy overcame her shyness and insecurities and kicked ass from the very beginning of the contest to inspire me to get the non-profit started. She is now a rock star, a real one.

I couldn't wait to call my friend Carine in Braffouéby to tell her the big news. I trusted her as my confidant and I wanted her to represent us, find a contractor, and communicate with the village and the new chief. The chief during my Peace Corps days had retired. Carine has a shrill tone in her voice and was ecstatic. She screamed for joy so loud on the phone that I was immediately forced to hold it away from my ear.

138

We had a registered 501c3 non-profit, Ivory Coast Mothers and Children, by 2008, thanks to a brilliant young friend, Marisa, who had non-profit experience and offered to help launch ICMC. Mike wound up paying for a good lawyer for us because we tried for a year and a half to wait for one pro-bono attorney, but that was taking way too long. She assembled a creative and experienced group of people for our Board of Directors and then organized a kickoff event at my nephew, Brian's bar to raise money and awareness.

Generous people began to donate to support the dream of a far-away chief in a small rural village in Africa whom they had never met. My sons stepped up with the talented, loving women in their lives, McKenzie and Amanda, and together with their friends and families, all donated to the auctions and raffles and bought tickets to our outrageously creative fund-raising parties, and graciously, held usually at one of Michael's fabulous places. Our success was built on the clever invitations, varied theme parties with costumes, great music, and ambiance. Shout out to McKenzie. Many fun and lively people attended and donated. I supplied the passion and people stepped up in ways I never imagined. There was also an anonymous super angel who donated $85,000 that gave us the extra boost we needed.

It was always the women who inspired me. I continued to ruminate about the babies born in homes in unsanitary conditions where infant mortality was high, living with no access to trained midwives or basic healthcare or disease prevention. My original concept was to construct a maternity center, but since the Ministry of Health wanted a full health clinic with an infirmary, we went forward cooperating with them for the goal of building a "semiprivate rural clinic."

"Why is this construction taking so long?" They had enough money.

"Why is it so difficult to receive a full accounting of the funding with receipts?"

"Why am I to act with a sense of urgency, and you are not?" All their requests were urgent which should have been a red flag.

The Return to Côte d'Ivoire

The goal of ICMC was to improve maternal and general health by building a clinic in Braffouéby. My son, Matthew, offered to accompany me back to the village for the first time in over seven years to meet the new chief of the village and my friend Carine who had been my friend and the go-between when sending money for the construction of the clinic.

I was full of hope from the hype about meeting the much-heralded new chief at our hotel in Abidjan, where Matt and I were staying to recuperate from our 23-hour plane trip and inevitable jet lag. The young, charismatic chief made a grand entrance standing tall and resplendent in his meticulous, heavily embroidered full-length grand boubou made with the highest quality *pagne*, speaking elegant French to introduce himself and to welcome us before our much-anticipated arrival in the village. I immediately understood why the village was so anxious to make him chief. He had an incredible presence and was already employed as a functionary in the state government. His plan was to spend long weekends in Braffouéby and to commute an hour and a half to work on Monday afternoons after the Monday morning village meetings. The bright new modern chief used words like "transparency" and spoke about his plans for progress and prosperity in the village. He was well-educated and appeared to have every quality of an ideal leader and role model. I was sold and optimistic. The old guard was now passé, and the future was with him.

The weekly village meetings are always a thorn in my side because the women are excluded, although I am invited during each trip for them to welcome me and for me to report the nature of my visit. When I was living there, however, I would be invited to share my project goals or issues from time to time. Maybe now, with a new chief, I thought, that women would have a chance to participate if they wanted, but it never happened. Women are discriminated against and are largely excluded from high-paying jobs, ownership of land, and political posts. Women's rights are human rights, it was said by Hilary Clinton at the United Nations Conference on Women in Beijing. Thankfully, gender equality is part of the Sustainable Development Goals, but it will go on deaf ears in the small villages in Africa where men rule.

It felt like an eternity since I left that early morning in 2002 with my sister, Janet, on our way to Ghana, and I was jumping out of my skin to see everyone again and witness the progress of the clinic since we had already sent hefty sums of money to Carine. Their half-assed attempts at accounting for it would be corrected on this trip.

Three cars loaded with my old friends from Braffouéby greeted us at the hotel in Abidjan to escort us back to the village. What a warm welcome! However, it was odd to see the villagers in cars, especially since almost nobody owned one when I was there last. As our entourage drove down the old bumpy road to enter the village, a cacophony of trumpets and fanfare filled the air playing joyful marching tunes. I was overwhelmed with warmth from the love, and the heat, as we were greeted with animated cheers, and friendly, familiar faces along with American and Ivorian miniature flags vigorously waving everywhere. My face flooded with tears.

We went directly to where the chairs were carefully arranged for the speeches in front of a grandstand with a gigantic American flag draped next to an Ivorian flag as the backdrop. After the program of speeches filled with messages of welcome and gratitude, we toured the clinic's raw structure. I was stunned by the fact that there was so much more work left to be done after almost 2 years of sending money. I was shocked because the government had already paid for the foundation, which was part of the agreement, and there was little else to see except crude cement blocks which could have been built in four days. I was given every excuse.

We were invited to a dinner in the home of a prestigious family with other special guests where we feasted on *foutou, attiéké* and sauces made of *agouti*, chicken, and lamb. During the meal, little children crawled around under my table to peek at Matthew and me, and nearby, I could see more little heads poking through the railings of the security gate. They were curious and also wanted some food, of course, so I handed them whatever I had under the table and through the post openings, much to the disapproval of Carine.

"Go away, children! Get out of here!" she barked and clucked at them and then afterward, she flashed her warm winning smile at Matthew and me.

The celebration was excessive for people living in poverty, although heartwarming, and I wondered out loud how they were paying for the enormous display of hoopla.

When I asked Carine, "What is up with the building?"

I was told while shaking her head in disgust, "You know how things move slowly around here."

I laughed mostly out of nervousness but was assured that the materials were already purchased with the tens of thousands of dollars we had already sent. She explained that it was difficult to find competent workers. I believed her.

Matt is curious and playful. I was happy to see him soak up the culture and roll with the many new experiences. He had studied in France and had a facility for the language and most importantly, he wasn't timid about speaking. The children loved him, especially the soccer players. Since his visit, on my following trips, he always makes sure that I am equipped with enough regulation soccer balls for all the teams and for the school to enjoy. Watching Matt interact with everyone and immerse himself in the moments was a joy for me.

Matt stayed in the other tiny one-room house next to mine, which were both owned by Carine's brother. Each contained only a bed with an old thin foam mattress on boards and barred windows with no

142

glass and torn screens, and walls with decades-old faded and stained smurf blue paint jobs. When I woke up the first morning in my room, my whole back was swollen, red and itchy to the point of madness. Carine came over, threw out the mattress and arranged to have another slab of foam delivered, much to my appreciation. The local boutique sold a bug bomb called Rambo that I am sure was 100% carcinogens, but nonetheless, every night, we sprayed the heavy fog in our rooms.

Carine took it upon herself to command our every movement. She made our daily arrangements for meals and meetings and was angry if we chose to veer from her plans. Carine had our carefully prepared agenda so tightly scheduled that there was only the siesta after lunch when we were able to speak to someone who was not on her schedule.

"Mom, she is strange," Matt remarked to me with a quizzical look upon meeting her.

During the time I lived there, it was different. She had her opinions about everything, but I paid little attention. I was there on a mission as a volunteer, and I really didn't care much about what she thought and admittedly, I was entertained by the fact that she was such a strong and singular character.

Carine drove Matt and me to another clinic in Elibou the next day that serves a much larger population to hopefully glean some ideas from them. They have been supported over many years by a generous group of people from the south of France called AMSAF. We joined their meeting that droned on for hours and much of the time they were speaking Abidgi if not French. It had been a while since I had spoken or heard any French or Abidgi and I missed many of their conversations and basically, barely caught the gist. During the long, drawn-out meeting, Matt amused himself by observing the different personalities and he didn't appear at all to be bored.

It was inspiring to see an established, well-run rural clinic and I couldn't wait to get ours started in our own village At night Matthew drank some *koutoukou, bangi* and chewed the khat leaves, hanging out with the men to "better understand the culture," as he explained. I pointed out to him nearby where a palm tree was tipped on its side which was where the men retrieved their latest supply of *bangi*. Somehow, Matt and I managed to create some free time to explore the village and catch up with old friends in Braffouéby away from Carine. We even went inside of the house I lived in during Peace Corps.

Boniface from the village took Matthew and me on a tour of some of the new "hevea" plantations. The current market offered a hefty profit for the rubber crop at that time. A new rubber tree takes seven years before it is ready to make money at the market. There was a mild frenzy going on about everyone wanting to get in on the action. The problem was that people gave up their vital food gardens and planted the hevea trees instead in order to try and cash in on the bonanza. Seven years later, the market became glutted. Not only were people looking at higher prices for food because of the sudden lack of individual gardens, but the prices for *hevea* had dropped to almost nothing close to what they had expected and unfortunately, there was little profit. Adding to their problems, the soil is not fertile for planting another crop after *hevea* cultivation for another 5 years due to resulting poor soil conditions. The climate was changing and less predictable, with drought-like seasons becoming more frequent. Food scarcity is exacerbated by climate change, inflation and sadly, people giving up their own vegetable gardens.

The new Chief Koffi, the high hope of the future, drove up in a rambling old red car one afternoon to pick me up and drive me to Dabou to try to bolster up some more support from the hierarchy of the Ministry of Health during my visit. It was a noble gesture.

The route was especially bumpy through the dense woods as he pointed out some government-built foundations for new village clinics that were supposed to be completed and to be opened by the different impoverished communities. It was alarming to see the structures

144

already overgrown with weeds, a disturbing reminder that the villages were given little money from the government for healthcare, and the inhabitants were unable to support the different projects.

The Chief said with a warm smile, looking over at me, "You know, all of these other villages don't have Patricia to help them."

The chief a couple years later replaced that old red car with a shiny new black Land-Rover. He asked me once if I thought he had rebuilt his house and bought his new car with ICMC money. It was very early on in his term, but I was so stunned by the question that I just laughed it off. When would I learn that I should not ignore my nervous fake laugh?

Despite the slow progress, I believed that the clinic had turned a corner and it was the beginning of better health for the village. We sent a container of medical supplies and equipment in 2011 through the Hospital Sisters Mission Outreach in Joliet, Illinois, before the grand opening. I couldn't wait to see the transformation and was anxious for the next visit after the delivery.

Figure 23 Welcome back festivities

Figure 24 the backdrop at the welcome ceremony

145

Figure 25 Matthew with his new village crew

The Children's Struggles

The first baby was finally born and celebrated joyfully in the Patricia Nau Clinic (named after my mother) in May of 2013. Hallelujah chorus of angels! It took five long years from when we first organized and received our 501c3 document. The new baby happened to be a relative of Carine's.

There were few disease preventative measures to stay healthy when I arrived as a volunteer. The tradition before a meal was to pass around a bowl of water that you would dip your hands into and then pass it on to the next person, along with the towel.

The water from the stream was orangey colored like the soil, with unrecognizable oily debris floating on top. Wet clothing was normally set on the ground to dry nearby. Because of the dirty, unfiltered water filled with microbes, the majority of the people had worms. When I lived there, a woman from an international aid organization came to test the people for worms and pass out anti-parasitic medications. She explained to me that worms made them more susceptible to other infections and diseases and that some common symptoms are abdominal pain, diarrhea, anemia and nutritional deficiencies which can cause organ damage.

There is now clean filtered water at the clinic and for the neighbors since we built a cistern available to all. People used to wash their clothes and children played in the murky shallow stream that wrapped half way around the village. The good news is that no child is swimming in the stream, nor are the women washing clothes in the stream anymore, plus the women are more likely to hang up their clothes since there is now an enlightened awareness about bacteria.

The families and children in the schools became sensitized to the importance of hand washing with soap and water thanks to the 80 new classroom sinks that ICMC installed with the help of Johnson & Johnson's Caring Crowd fundraising platform. The young girls used to be the ones delegated every morning to go to the well and bring back a bucket of water balanced on their heads for use during the school day which caused problems in the development of their young necks early on in life. The well water was much cleaner than the stream but not filtered from impurities.

The people of Braffoueby and Bécedi were way ahead of the curve during the pandemic because hand washing with soap and water was already customary. Hand washing with soap is now practiced at a young age and remains to be the most economical way to prevent diseases.

Figure 26 Hand washing in each classroom

Figure 27 Young girls carrying the daily water from the well

Figure 28 Cistern for clean, filtered water

Opportunities for children in poverty are exceedingly limited, as their education is impacted by corruption, compounded further by extreme income inequality, thus deepening the extent of poverty. I was troubled by the idea that a young man who had never passed his final tests after high school petitioned our non-profit to pay someone off who is affiliated with the Ivorian school system so that he could be hired as an elementary school teacher. Many young people, the most vulnerable and disadvantaged, are receiving an inferior education in schools with crowded classrooms, poorly maintained facilities, lack of supplies, including books and chalk for the blackboards, and most importantly, many low-quality, often absent teachers.

Since textbooks are rare for students, few people have any lighting to be able to study their notes after class in the evenings. Now that some of the villages have street lighting, many young people meet outside under the light where only the most serious students at that age would truly study.

Most families require that their young girls help with the daily tasks. She gathers wood, fetches water, minds the siblings, works in the fields, washes clothes, sweeps the courtyard, and along the way, she unwittingly attracts a young man that makes her pregnant. If we could improve access to quality education or skills training, maybe the girls would be empowered to make better choices.

An energetic middle-aged woman, Madame Kré, takes care of scores of children because she took it upon herself to open her home and provide the basics for orphaned children who had no one to care for them in the village, including giving them love and discipline. Madame is also the mother of our two doctors who work at the clinic, Félix and Marc.

The main room of her large swept clean, cement home has rolled-up mats for sleeping lined up along the walls where the wall-to-wall children lay out their mats on the floor at night. The children started clapping their hands to a bright song she taught them the moment Anna from NYU and I arrived to pass out gifts of new clothes and school supplies.

Many more orphaned children are cared for by other Abidgi women no matter how impoverished they are themselves, because the tribe strongly believes in the value of each child. Sagne, who works at the high school and in the past for a non-profit for HIV/AIDS support, helped ICMC identify the children in Braffouéby and Sikensi who were living with different families. Some of the children did not have birth certificates because of the expense.

ICMC initiated another project with Sagne to distribute medical cards with a history of their vaccinations for the school children in Braffouéby and Sikensi. They also received check-ups. Unfortunately, we underestimated the number of children needing treatments at the time for malnutrition, anemia or who were suffering from one of the tropical diseases. There were simply not enough resources available at the time to treat each child.

There are four children born at the clinic with Cerebral Palsy who require extensive therapies at a school in Bonua, far from the village. The children suffer from a neurologic disability that affects their body movements, muscle tone and posture. They also need special schools, shoes, equipment and medications. ICMC raises money with them in mind. Little Rose has shown tremendous improvements over the years. Samuel requires support because his grandmother is caring for him and is HIV positive. She is afraid she will die, and the child will have nobody.

Honorine had meningitis which sadly left her crippled after ICMC provided intensive care for her in Abidjan and occasionally helped with her school expenses and food. She had no way to attend high school since her village was miles away and there was no transport provided for the students to attend the one high school serving all 15 villages spread out for miles. Sadly, Honorine recently died from complications and anemia. She was so exceedingly bright but became despondent over having difficulty attending school. Transport to school seems so basic to Americans.

There was nothing more sorrowful than attending one of the funerals for a baby or a child and the sight of a grieving mother on her knees in agony. Every child is a treasure. With prenatal care at the clinic, which was initially a hard sell to pregnant women, many more babies are born healthy. Soon they will offer ultrasound which alerts the mother and midwife about a potentially complicated birth where she would need to prepare to give birth at a hospital equipped with blood supplies and oxygen.

The most dangerous time for a child is between ages 1 and 5 years old. Poverty is associated with their shorter life expectancy and also the diseases that are caused by insufficient quantity and quality of food. The insidious cycle of poverty continues as poor health follows poverty which is why 80 children die per 1000 births in the Ivory Coast. However, the high numbers in the last 20 years have improved because of the important attention to the Millennium Development Goals. Malaria should be halved through their efforts by the end of the decade, which would be transformational.

There is little chance of success for those young people born into poverty because of the many obstacles and circumstances that face them along the way. A young man from the village attended brigadier training which was paid for by ICMC. After a year, he was still fighting to get paid after landing a job. The head commander's first excuse was that he had never seen the cadet before. It was later discovered that the commander was holding all of the money while attempting to flee to Europe and was arrested at the border. The newer established rule is that the brigadier must now work a month before getting paid. He has already invested in the proper uniform plus many other fees and training, just for the privilege of working. How is the young man to survive without a salary? And now there is a whole newly formed brigade, and he needs $642 to be able to work there. The story sounds outrageously unjust to me.

When a young man applied for a job at a large beer company, he was required to pay around $100 for an identification card and wear proper clothes and boots. He was soon laid off from work. A new large successful company bought out the original company where he was working with a new requirement to purchase another ID card for $129. In both cases, he was faced with working a day rate for barely enough to eat.

In higher education, there is an endless request for payment for "documents," which is another way for the professor to make money instead of the students buying textbooks. The teacher makes the required Xerox copies of textbooks and sells them to the students. It is rarely specified up front how many "documents" will be needed for the course. What I call the "document racket" makes it difficult for ICMC or anyone else to budget the needed expenses. If a person has money, they will most likely be educated and find a job, usually bought through their connections and payment of upfront fees.

Figure 29 Typical village classroom

Figure 30 New benches donated by my cousin, Chas

The Inauguration of the Clinique Patricia Nau

Marisa Swyston was the original Executive Director of ICMC and taught me the ropes about managing a non-profit. I had invited my son, Mike, to attend the inauguration of the clinic in 2014, but he was kind enough to donate the money for Marisa to attend instead. Hyped as being quite an affair with invitations sent out to all the chiefs in the surrounding fifteen villages along with dignitaries from the Ministry of Health in Abidjan, we were highly anticipating the trip. They had a ceremony with speeches and a brass band, with every village chief attending adorned in their formal gold jewelry, ornate golden crowns on their heads, and wearing their finest colorful *boubous* made of *pagne* elegantly embellished with thick gold embroidery. The chiefs of the village were resplendent in their golden crowns, necklaces, and bracelets.

Before the event, Marisa and I were invited to visit the Braffouéby chief's home, which he had rebuilt to resemble a Trump-style penthouse. There was gold everywhere. The Chief sat proudly on his lavish golden throne-like chair arranged near his wife's mini throne who was proudly smiling as we sat in awe of our garish surroundings. Marisa, Carine, and I were seated on upholstered armchairs with ornate gold embellishments that formed a crown at the top of the chairs which gave a very regal appearance to anyone seated. The chairs were lined up under a window draped with gold fringe on swags of heavy fabric with draped cornices also with fringe. Carine was dressed to kill in iridescent pink and purple with plenty of gold embroidery complete with gold jewelry. She accompanied us wherever we went and was verbally upset after the ceremonies when nobody mentioned her name in a speech, including me. Apparently, she believed that she was the one who asked that the clinic be built.

For the ceremony, Marisa and I were seated in two chairs facing the crowd as everyone assembled. The new mothers lined up with their tiny babies, who were all born in the clinic. One by one, the proud mamas came up to the front showing off their sweet, healthy bundles for us to hold and to admire. I was weeping from the experience. Afterward, they gifted us with lovely long dresses made from *pagne*, and gold bracelets with matching necklaces, earrings, and furry animal flip flops. The grateful mothers with their shining, happy faces were all the gifts that we needed. Marisa left soon after the celebration with her *cadeaux*, "Godspeed" from the villagers, and the knowledge that she had made a difference in their lives.

153

There was a drifter who I spotted when I dropped off my loot and said good-bye to Marisa. He kept watching me from behind a tree and then attempted several times to approach me, but I refused to spend any time with him. I told him that he needed to meet with the chief first, following protocol. I never reported the incident, unfortunately, so he broke into where I was staying and stole all my gifts and my computer. I was relieved that Marisa had already left, so her celebration was not tarnished. The village was outraged upon hearing the news. The multitudes came over for support while teams of young men set out to capture the thief. Later, the Chief summoned me to his home again, where he presented me with newly purchased gifts while they repaired the door and the locks.

Figure 31 Mathers lining up with gifts for us

Figure 32 Inauguration Day

Jamie and Diana of Tremble Productions

On two trips in 2010 and 2015, I traveled with my talented friends, who I had met at work selling phones. The creative team, Jamie and Diana, arrived fully equipped to make a professional video and interview many of the women who documented their experiences before and after the clinic was built. The second trip in 2015, they traveled with 17 pieces of luggage that included a drone which stirred up levels of fascination and curiosity that were off the charts. We again stayed in the tiny one-room houses of Carine's brother with the sprawling backyard where they worked diligently throughout the day and the evenings on the videos, and we drank beer and laughed and told stories most of the nights while they organized their work schedule and we formulated a plan for the interviews.

Jamie pointed out to me that Carine was a mean woman in the way she disrespects her employees. I should have listened again to my own little voice, Matthew and Jamie, and Diana, all shared the same opinion, but I continued to believe in her. Carine insisted that we eat at her place for all three meals, which was always delicious, and she was ready on the spot to pick us up in her car. My friends, on the other hand, were firm about going over to Carine's only once a day, no matter how tasty her food was. I followed their wishes, much to the displeasure of the bossy one. I never again stayed in one of the tiny houses.

Figure 33 Jamie and Diana in Abidjan before their first visit

Figure 34 From the top of the "rocher" Jamie, Diana with Willie
viewing the treetops

The Betrayal

I was in bed at home in Chicago close to midnight late in 2015. The phone rang from an unknown New York phone number which I normally would never answer, but I had an uneasy feeling that there was trouble somewhere. It was Bamba. I was introduced to him at one of Carine's sumptuous luncheon events that she had arranged during a visit. Bamba was prosperous and owned a home and land in Braffouéby that he farmed, and a home in New York where he lived with his family.

He said that he had recently returned from a trip to the village and began the conversation with, "The information that I am going to give you was kept from you because of your relationship with Carine." I listened while he regurgitated the whole ugly story. I was devastated and felt ill when he described the poor condition of the building, the story of how the women were staying away from the clinic, and how Carine would drop in during the day to scream at the staff and insult them about how they didn't know what they were doing. I was surprised and outraged when I heard that people were ordered never to speak to me unless they were approved by Carine, and that she organized my visits so that nobody would tell me anything that Carine didn't want me to hear.

I responded, "All of this is too much information for me to grasp right now and I will have to call you back." I did not sleep that night.

I knew I had to discuss this issue with my friends Kevin and Margaret, who were always there to help me sort out various situations. The good thing about Kevin was that he has an excellent memory and has given me sage, useful advice since the very onset. He has been my trusted mentor.

That evening we decided to invite Bamba to Chicago for the following weekend at Kevin's suggestion. ICMC offered to buy Bamba's airfare, meals, and a hotel room and we were happy that he agreed to come. I made his arrangements. He arrived in a few days.

Bamba told us about the shoddy contractor, who was Carine's friend, and the chief who I originally trusted but had become disillusioned with because of his lack of communication. Bamba knew how much money I had wired Carine because he oversaw the invoices that I regularly sent him in the past to double-check the bills Carine sent me. Bamba and another trusted person from Abidjan both agreed when they checked the invoices that the village should be quite pleased that they chose to use only the best materials available. Bamba surmised where the money was really going, to the chief and to Carine and not for the quality materials. There was gross mismanagement of the funds.

I was crushed by the news about how Carine would show up at the clinic and shout orders at everyone, criticize, diminish, and denigrate, which was believable because I knew how she treated her own workers over the years. Carine was the trusted one, my friend, who was supposed to manage the money we sent. She was the one responsible for paying the staff and contractor, informing the chief about the progress or issues. I offered to pay her but she said that she would never take any payment from ICMC for her work because the clinic meant so much to her.

When Bamba arrived in Chicago the following weekend, I met him at the Hilton Airport Hotel to have dinner. We talked about his trip, his family, and anything else except the elephant in the room. The following day I picked him up to enjoy a steak at Gibson's for lunch and then went back to my place to introduce him to my closest friends and support system so he could tell the group exactly what he saw and what he knew.

I heard how utterly demoralizing she was to the whole medical team. The women in the village stopped coming in for prenatal care or to have their babies at the clinic because they didn't trust anyone there. They did not want to support the hostile environment and they believed Carine was a thief. The building itself was falling to ruin. There was too much painful information to assimilate, but I continued to listen carefully, feeling heartsick to my core. Nothing was as I thought it to be. I was overcome with deep despair upon hearing the details of the impossible situation.

Why was I so blind? The truth was too much for me to bear. My head was now out of the sand. I not only disappointed the entire village but my flawed ability to judge people accurately failed the kind individuals who generously donated to establish the clinic. It was clear that my best friend in the village, Carine, and the new Chief Koffi were scammers. Unfortunately, they compromised the construction and the management of the clinic for their own personal gain. I unwittingly believed that the clinic would flourish and that progress was on the way. All money came to a dead halt.

"How would we ever restore faith in our work?" I kept repeating to myself while engulfed in a storm of hopelessness.

The chief was accused of using funds from the Chinese and from ICMC. The village had agreed to the Chinese proposal of allowing them in the village to extract granite from the surrounding hills, although not the spiritual hill, the *Rocher*. The crews used super-sized extractors and cranes to mine and blast the raw granite from the mini mountains with the promise that the impossible roads would be repaired and school classrooms refurbished, and I was told that there would also be financial support for the clinic. None of which ever happened. The people suffered from the monster-sized trucks that entered the village, creating dust and dirt bombs all over their homes and in their lungs while they blasted the granite hills with dynamite. Oscar especially has suffered from the dust since his lungs are weak because of his inability to move his body from polio. Not surprisingly, it was said that a large portion of the funds from them went to the chief and his cohorts.

After the betrayal, I carried on in a positive manner when I needed to and did my best to continue telling uplifting stories about how much of a difference the clinic was making in the village. It was sometimes difficult for me to hold on to the belief that we must continue to support the people who worked there and especially, for those in need of healthcare.

"People are not investing in a fantasy, and we will work this out somehow," I kept repeating to myself. "We shall overcome."

I couldn't talk about how we had to rework all the electricity and plumbing or how we had to have the roof and the ceilings repaired because of those two people. The skimpy tiling was already in need of repair. I had to project a positive image so that the good people in Braffouéby would win and so that friends of ICMC would continue to donate. I regained full trust in our mission after meeting Theresa.

Allyson and Theresa

The next day after Bamba left, I offered my bright and ambitious friend, Allyson, a position on our Board of Directors that she immediately accepted. She called me back the same day to say, "As my first official duty as a Board member, I want to introduce you to Theresa."

Allyson's friend had a successful for-profit business in India, Work+Shelter, who she believed would be a good resource for me. They both accepted my invitation the same evening to come over for cocktails on my mini terrace in the Ukrainian Village. Theresa swooped in like a whirlwind of energy and light. She had graduated from the University of Michigan and worked at Google in New York and then left her sought-after position because she wanted to dig into something that made a difference in the world.

I began telling them both my intense and arduous story trying unsuccessfully to keep my composure. I spilled the full truth along with my tears about what was happening in Braffouéby. Theresa was tracking everything I said, and then she stated that she would go with me in two weeks to confront the Chief and my former best friend, Carine. She was convinced that we would find a solution. I felt a ray of hope. As fate would have it, another friend had just canceled her trip with me two days before, so I was grateful and elated that together we would travel to the village and make things right.

Theresa worked with me to create a system of accountability, transparency, and communication with a new management team, complete with job descriptions. She restored my faith in our work. Most importantly, she helped me find the courage and strength it took to face those who tried to take away the hope that the women in the village originally held on to so that they could deliver their babies in a safe, clean, functioning medical facility and have healthcare for their families, in a clinic operated with integrity by people who cared for them.

I would no longer stay at Carine's brother's shabby place, nor were we under her control anymore after I was made aware of the chicanery. In fact, I did not even let Carine know that we were arriving.

Bamba arranged for us to stay at the home of Blaise, a successful accountant in Abidjan, who warmly welcomed us into his fine second home in the village with his enthusiastic cook, Aisha, who prepared our delicious meals outdoors on the open fire. It was a safe and happy place, roomy and clean, with blue and white polar bear sheets on our beds and surrounded by a cement security fence and, most of all, kind and supportive people to welcome us.

I asked the Chief to call a meeting at his place soon after we arrived with Carine and his thirty-five or so yes-men for our day of reckoning. Theresa had prepared me with the new set of guidelines, and we were "fired up and ready to go," as Obama used to say.

Everyone gathered in the chief's brand new spacious meeting area next to his gilded house. He greeted the attendees and then declared, "The buck stops with me," clearly taking full responsibility for the functioning of the clinic. He then gave me the floor.

I stood up with my knees quivering in anger and fear but resolute as I first glanced at Theresa, my rock, and then directly into the chief's eyes. I made the first non-negotiable demand, clearly stating that Carine and the Chief must relinquish their association with the clinic, or ICMC would leave the village forever. I could hear gasps echoing around the room while my face continued to burn red hot.

I followed up with, "Morale of the staff is at an all-time low. I saw water that has been leaking in the treatment room on moldy boxes of medical supplies, which we sent you! You obviously didn't care enough to have the ceiling fixed or even have the boxes moved out of the way, opened, or organized. In fact, it has been reported that you have never even visited the clinic yourself! And you are in charge?"

He responded, "I'll pay for the ceiling to be repaired."

I shot back, "Both you and Carine failed us and the village."

I looked over at Carine, who was speechless for the first time in her life.

I let them know that we had formed a new management team who would regularly report to ICMC and that Oscar would be in charge as the new Director.

I finished with, "Only if you agree to our terms will we stay. Otherwise, we are out."

I heard more rumbling and then one of the men across the room called Oscar a "petit" because of his handicap.

At that moment, I slammed my notebook closed and glared at them, but went on to say, "We have been ignored except for you asking for more money, and despite my multiple requests for proper accounting, we have received for the most part, a stone wall, which is not acceptable."

I looked over at Theresa after I spoke my piece. She discreetly shot me a "let's get the hell out of here" look and together we walked out the door to find a big surprise.

A large group of my now grown-up kids who used to gather at my house in the village during the evenings had assembled out on the road to blow whistles, bang the drums, and make a ruckus. A '60s-style protest was in full swing, which was a spectacular and gratifying sight. The crowd held up homemade signs that read, "Where is the money?" "You all are thieves!" "Save our clinic!"

It was heart-warming to see Oscar at the demonstration in his wheelchair with many of the little children I knew from years ago who were now young adults. I hadn't even told Oscar yet that he would be appointed the new Director. The cheers and support were overwhelming. Also, it was a relief that the young people had sent a car to wait for us to whisk us away down the road to Blaise's house. Theresa and I immediately hopped in, hung out the windows, and waved at the crowd while blowing kisses and giving them all big thumbs up.

After winding down from the battle, safe and sound at Blaise's feeling a release from the emotionally depleting experience, there was a knock on the door. I opened it to find Carine standing there. She began screaming and flecking her spittle at me the second she saw me and ranted on about how I "dirtied her name" and on and on with her tirade until I finally closed the door in her face.

My only retort was, "You dirtied your own name."

I heard her peel out of the driveway in her car, only later to find out that she had broken into the village home of Bamba, my friend, where she stole his pepper spray. Armed with her weapon, she tracked down another friend of mine, Claude, and ambushed him near his home by spraying the mace directly in his face.

Claude was upset and in pain when he came over to report what had happened to him. Carine had never wanted Claude to be included in any of our ICMC projects, probably because of her twisted sense of right and wrong. He was short, balding and stuttered, highly intelligent, has a heart of gold and cares deeply about being involved in something significant. He is presently employed at the mayor's offices in Sikensi where I am sure, he is contributing immensely to the betterment of the area.

Our host gave us a security detail before I even thought about us ever being in danger, and since that day, we have never ventured out anywhere from Blaise's house without our big strong, handsome security man, Ghislain.

The chief's meeting was the last time I ever saw that man whom I had trusted to be the "new savior" of the village. It is said that the former chief stealthily returns from time to time to visit his home after nightfall when nobody is around to see him. The cathartic reckoning was the actual beginning of Chief Koffi's loss of power.

And I have since learned that Carine has never set foot in her own village again nor have I ever seen her. Unfortunately, the incident divided her family, but all of them have continued to be courteous and kind to me.

Figure 35 Theresa with the children

The New Director

Leadership was key for us to continue our work. I knew that Oscar didn't know anything about healthcare or management at the time, but he was astute, possessed organizational skills and there was nobody more competent or trustworthy, I believed. Oscar, as Director, had the enormous task of working with the medical team through the challenges of elevating clinic standards, revitalizing low morale, and enhancing clinic experience. Additionally, he was faced with managing all the necessary repairs in the clinic, one project at a time. He accepted his role to help lead the discouraged healthcare team and to strive for excellence. Together they have achieved that goal, having been named the best clinic in the region by the Ministry of Health at least five times in a row.

Oscar's first disease prevention mission was to build a cistern for fresh, clean, filtered water to be available to the clinic and to the neighbors. He came up with ingenious ways to circumvent the Ministry of Health and suffer their wrath to make our budgets go further and offer more services for the patients. The staff opened a pharmacy and a laboratory, built an incinerator and a cistern for filtered water, hired a head of sanitation, and kept the doors open 24/7 with night security.

Oscar is genuinely empathetic and has had the impossible task of deciding who is most in need of aid of scholarships, malnourishment, cerebral palsy, orphaned children, cancer or other diseases like malaria and typhoid, surgeries, education, or whatever issue is the most pressing. He is made aware of how much funding is available that month or for special appeals by ICMC through social media and emails for special funding. The people speak to him because he is the liaison between ICMC and the village including the clinic. He carries the load since his responsibility was to make budgets and account for the funds. Ruben whose father was deeply loved by all and who met an untimely death is now assisting him. Oscar, is acutely aware that everyone's issues cannot be supported. ICMC's original, very ambitious idea was to never turn anyone away at the clinic. The intention of providing care for everyone worked for a while but would have been impossible to continue because we never had the funding like St. Jude

Hospital. Presently, the local team called COGES assists in recommending the distribution of any special funding beyond the salaries.

Since many people cannot afford to pay even the minimal $.50 consultation fee, the clinic is not sustainable. The staff keeps track of those who cannot pay in a thick notebook and does their best to care for every person who visits. Some people are only able to pay a portion, or make sporadic payments, or not at all. The notebook is a visual reminder of the existing poverty impacting people's lives and acts as a wearying reminder for ICMC to never give up.

During Oscar's two-year studies at the university, he made some outstanding friends in the medical field who have come to our aid many times with discounted surgeries and consultations. We are indebted to his doctor friends, especially Dr. Maxime Koffi, and appreciate their compassion and excellent care they have provided.

The clinic's number one challenge was persuading the women to come in for prenatal care and to garner trust in the professionally trained midwife who was not from their tribe. It was a hard sell because the original midwife was aloof and indifferent, as was apparent from my very first meeting. She fancied stylish outfits, wore make-up, dolled up hairdos and stood around posing with a cell phone in her hand when few people in the village owned one at the time. She looked me over but didn't waste a minute to let me know how busy she has been, which was doubtful because I saw for myself in the journals how many women had visited, the numbers were low.

The women did not relate to her, nor did I. Mercifully, she was replaced after a couple of years. It was an uphill battle for the newer midwife to earn the village women's trust, and it did not happen overnight. The women had to be convinced that prenatal, post-natal care and vaccinations were essential to their health and for that of the newborns. The community was pleased with her replacement, Reine, because of the new midwife's skills, resourcefulness, sincerity, and positive attitude. ICMC is proud to say that all the babies are now born at our clinic with a professionally trained midwife.

Figure 36 Oscar with new computer

Dr. Matt, Laura, Tammy

There was chaos when hundreds of people lined up in the village at daybreak after hearing the news that they could receive either prescription glasses, reading glasses, or sunglasses, including an eye exam from Dr. Matt. The good Dr. Matthew Gifford, Optometrist, with the help of his wife, Laura, and Tammy who works in Chicago with children's glasses traveled to the village for the gift of better vision for hundreds of women, men, and children. The challenge was to process all the people in an orderly and efficient manner when they were desperate, longing for the opportunity to undergo an eye exam. Since Dr. Matt and Laura had made numerous visits to other South American sites before, they were able to provide a sense of order and organization amidst the impending chaos. However, there were unpleasant outbursts from the crowd when I made the executive decision that older people should be seen first to protect them from the hot sun and then there were more loud protests when I thought we should see the schoolchildren during their mid-day break. I wanted to hide.

When the electricity didn't work and the Dr. couldn't use his machine to accurately measure their prescriptions, he had to give them out manually. It was hot and tempers flared except for the in control, ever-patient Dr. and his wife.

One evening after a long arduous day at the clinic, we all relaxed with a drink as Tammy had her hair cornrowed by one of the local stylists. It took hours to complete but lasted on her head for not more than ten minutes because of the excruciating pain that it caused. Young girls learn to sit still and somehow become habituated to the tortuous hairdos at a very young age. But mainly in the village, many mothers shave the children's heads because they believe that it is cleaner. I admit that years before I tried to wear the same kind of painful braids, but I too ripped them out as fast as possible, especially after I got a glance in the mirror. I was no Bo Derek.

Figure 37 Dr. Matt giving an eye exam

Kathy

In 2019, I met a young, high-energy, redheaded woman, Kathy, all dressed up with a big smile and bright, red-orange lipstick ready for a night out on the town. I was in a shared Uber with her on my way to a fundraiser for somebody else where Kathy and I immediately connected and shared some laughs. She happened to mention her interest in underserved areas of the world and that she was a pharmacist at a local hospital which immediately set off an internal alert. I invited her to join me on my upcoming trip to the Ivory Coast and she instantly agreed! It was a 10-minute Uber ride that had lasting consequences because not only did she carry along two whole suitcases filled with medical supplies and baby clothes, but she has since become a contributing member of our Board of Directors.

I told Kathy about an invitation to attend a STEM conference with Jeanette who worked at the World Bank in DC and is part of the Ivorian diaspora. We would travel by car up to the rural northern part of the country as guests, and she agreed that she would like to go.

We set off from Abidjan after our 23-hour plane journey, and a night in a hotel to recover. We met Jeanette for lunch to get to know her a bit, and then departed the next day to Bibita in a comfortable car on the modern main highway, initially, and then travelled over the bumpy rollercoaster roads that eventually took us to our remote destination. I was grateful that Kathy was a pharmacist because she had brought along some magic anti-nausea pills that I believed saved my life, as the driver cautiously navigated the rural, treacherous road.

The event was a demonstration/cultural festival with singing and dancing attended by activists and other hard-working women who were eager to share their daily challenges. They spoke about how the land is rich and produces bountiful crops, but many of the laborers in the country needlessly suffer and continue to go hungry. We would attest to the fact that the infrastructure is poor. It was evident that the population has the impossible task of getting the goods to market before rotting in the ground. The impressive group of women held the conference to campaign and organize for a better life. Two years later, in 2021, ICMC began collaborating with the World Bank and when I asked Jeannette if she had anything to do with this, she answered with, "It was about time".

Figure 38 Kathy holding a newborn

Figure 39 Kathy rearranging the pharmacy

Anna

Anna Erlandson traveled with me three times to the village. My friend, Pam, originally from the Indiana Dunes gave me a call that she was in town, and wanted me to meet her daughter, Anna. I hadn't seen either one of them in years since they had moved away to Oregon where Pam had opened a book store, A Children's Place. She said that Anna's goal was to spend some more time in Africa before applying for her master's degree program in Public and Global Health at New York University.

169

They came over for dinner and I had a running slide show playing on the TV in the background to help entice her, which was hardly necessary. When I invited her to travel with me, her eyes lit up. I don't know who was happier, Anna, her mother, or me? The village was the real winner. She is an all-star, and I was thrilled to have her on board.

During Anna's first trip, without hesitation she saw a situation in the maternity delivery room and asked for bleach and a scrub brush, got down on her knees and scoured every inch of the birthing table and the room, and then organized the storage room with newly purchased transparent bins we bought at the market in Sikensi. I followed her lead and put on the gloves too and gratefully pitched in under her direction. We found trash and sharps mixed in with supplies, and left-over bodily fluids underneath and on exam and delivery beds. It was disorganized and dirty. All supplies had been shoved into cabinets under the counters with no order, mixed in with soggy cardboard boxes and dirt in the drawers with lizards crawling out of the cabinet. She earned everyone's respect for setting a better standard of cleanliness and order. Her overall contribution has been enormous in raising funds and awareness during her role as President of ICMC in absentia.

On each trip we were able to get to know the clinic's staff better, including certain patients from the area. Anna and I received an invitation to the home of a very thin young mother with a contagious smile who had just delivered her eighth child, her only one at the clinic. The staff was completely charmed by her charismatic personality, and they made sure that the mother and baby had everything they needed, including clothing and medication. She lives deep in the forest outside the village with her young children and their "papa" who was blinded from an agricultural accident. Two of their older children had never been in school because they not only lived in extreme poverty, but their home was located too far away from any village school. We met "maman's" eldest very shy eight years old daughter, Madina, who could barely look me in the eye. Oscar recognized the need to educate their children, and he arranged for her to attend a boarding school through funding from ICMC. Madina did so well at the school that she skipped two grades and continues to be number one in her class. Now she stands tall and strong with a big smile and her younger brother follows the same stellar pattern.

When we visited the family, it was like traveling back to a time I had only imagined. A friend from Braffouéby drove us out towards the forest, and fortunately, they knew the way to their home down a long narrow curvy foot path, in the deep, dense, dark tropics. We finally arrived at the clearing where the mother and father were sitting surrounded by their children by a low fire. They were all as joyful, warm, and welcoming as she was. We brought the children some new clothing and a few balls, and watched them play. Even though they have never asked for anything, it is obvious there will be more children to sponsor for school.

Charlie, a young college age man, put together a GoFundMe page to build an incinerator on another trip with me and Anna. The children in the village don't have toys so when they find anything on the ground; they play with it. I remember looking out my window when I lived in Braffouéby and saw for myself what the kids had done with my trash. I cringed when I thought of what they would do with a syringe! The great thing about Charlie is that he was self-motivated to get the job done. He arose early every morning to help make cement to make the bricks with another worker Oscar had arranged for him. The incinerator was built without the approval from the Ministry of Health who had quoted many times more than what the cost Oscar had itemized on our own. The laboratory and the pharmacy were also established without permission for the same good reason, their quoted costs were too high. The outcome was that Oscar was hassled, but the goal was to provide the best services possible on the funds that we had available.

On another trip with Anna, she invited Dabney Close, also a NYU master's student, Emily, an emergency room nurse, and Joey, a medical scribe who will be a doctor one day. I was very pleased the young, energetic, highly professional team organized their own jam-packed agenda, aware of the goals we wanted to achieve. Together with the Ministry of Health they gave out 600 vaccinations with money raised from an ICMC fundraiser through a Johnson & Johnson Caring Crowd platform. Joey passed out colorful cartoon stickers to the tearful, just poked kids who suddenly burst into smiles, so proud of their new "badges".

The team and I ended the day touring three surrounding villages to do unannounced needs assessments. I took photos of my group's disturbed faces while they were exiting the neglected and impoverished clinics all in a state of disrepair. They lacked the basics. One site had no running water, and another didn't even have a stethoscope. I delicately mentioned to a nurse at one of the clinics, "Cleaning, and sweeping don't cost anything", which was not received very well. It was a grand gesture by the government to build the clinics years ago, but it was obvious that these neglected, impoverished, villages received little follow-up financial support for any type of health services.

The non-profit Vitamin Angels has truly been angels for the women and children, and they have aided in their disease prevention. We are grateful to them for donating over the years needed vitamin A, deworming meds, Vitamins for children ages 1-5 and ages 5-10 years, also prenatal vitamins for pregnant women in our village and for a neighboring village, Bécedi.

In Anna's Words

"I was fortunate enough to gain a strong understanding of the breadth of the issue of healthcare abroad, (in South Africa) but it was in Braffouéby that I could interact with the depth of the issues I am so committed to. I was able to take the past four years of studies and apply it to almost every interaction and decision I had the pleasure of being a part of. Yes, the experience was educational for me, but it was also reciprocated. I can only hope my contribution made a positive difference in the functionality of the Patricia Nau Clinic, but more importantly, I hope it is sustainable as I continue to work with Ivory Coast Mothers and Children in the field of global health."

Figure 40 Charlie making bricks with village coworker

Figure 41 Giving vaccinations with the Ministry of Health with Dabney, Anna, Emily and Joey

Figure 42 Our vaccination, needs assessment, and vitamin distribution team , Emily MacDonell, Anna Erlandson, me, Dabney Close, Joey Altermatt

Braffouéby Today

During the pandemic, the mothers were not carrying their babies in for check-ups and shots because of their fears of contamination. The staff came up with a solution of building an extra open-air side building where the two nurses, Theo and Patrick, give out vaccinations to the infants. The children are now physically separated from potentially infected people visiting the main building for consultations. The extension building has received considerable funding from the American Women for International Understanding (AWIU) to properly finish the floors, ceilings and add paint, along with other generous donations. The building also functions as a much-needed extra space for miscellaneous clinic business.

ICMC gave many scholarships, including law school, for a young girl who I knew when she was very young. Marie Laure said that she came home from school in fourth grade to find her mother dead and that she had never known her father. She was always melancholy because of her poverty and held little hope for her future. She was interviewed in one of the Jamie and Diana videos in 2010 and I remember how she tugged on our heartstrings. I hadn't heard any recent news from her and I finally contacted her. She was surviving by selling whatever she could for people on the street in Abidjan, earning less than $2 a day for her work. Initially, she asked ICMC to pay for baking school in Abidjan and requested an oven so she could make cakes and sell them in the market to support herself which we were happy to provide. Later she informed me that she was coming home one day from selling her cakes on the street and was assaulted by a woman in her neighborhood. She enclosed a horrific photo of herself with her broken collar bone and bruises all over her body. ICMC paid for her emergency care, and we located a women's group in Abidjan, "Etre une Femme," which provided necessary emotional counseling for her. When I followed up with her again to find out how she was healing, she revealed her desire to become a lawyer. I was so impressed with her ambition that I said yes before I knew the costs of the tuition, etc.

nor did I consult with anyone else. The school suggested that she move to a better law school in Bouaké after her first year, where she continued to excel. Jamie and Diana helped with her first year, my nephew, Nate, and his wife Amanda Franck paid for most of her second year, and my son Matthew and Amanda for most of her third year. She finished her third year and did well in class. She no longer carries the sadness but sees hope and promises for a better future, including her desire to help the orphans in Braffouéby. She is preparing for an internship which I hope will launch her career. Another calamity occurred when her new suit, required for her new job and computer were stolen from her apartment. ICMC did not replace the items that we had bought for her. The oven is gone too.

Blanche was part of the "4-kid group" with Willie, who knocked on my door early almost every morning in the village. She did exceptionally well in school and asked me if she could attend a highly regarded French hotel school in Abidjan. She performed well, as I expected from her because she is very bright. I was able to ask the owner of a hotel, the very lovely retreat Villa Mia, where we always stay in Abidjan, for her to complete her training as an intern. Her confidence level has soared and now she is employed at the same hotel and presently aims to be a teacher one day. The pay is minimal and she mainly performs housekeeping tasks, but she is employed.

School lunches keep kids in school and are best for disease prevention, of course malnutrition and especially anemia which worsens malaria symptoms and can induce a coma in the youngest children. ICMC buys the canned fish, palm oil and rice that they serve every day thanks to donations from AWIU and from friends of ICMC who have donated during events over the years. A couple of village women prepare the meals and clean up after, and they are paid a small sum for their generous work.

The medical staff, our doctors, Félix and Marc and our original nurse, Théo, speak the local language and understand and know the people, the Abidgi traditions and culture. Their contributions are monumental. People come from all over the region to see them because of their well-earned reputations for giving excellent care. They all have big, warm personalities that make people feel welcome. They refer patients to a hospital in Abidjan when they are unable to provide the care they need. Poverty makes it almost impossible to have most services and medical treatments within their reach which is when ICMC reaches out to find the funding.

It is customary that doctors, nurses, and midwives in the country are placed by the Ministry of Health at their discretion. The government pays the salaries of the nurses and midwives, but they say it is less than a living wage which is why ICMC provides supplements for them. The doctors, Felix and Marc Kré expressed an interest in working at our clinic, which is extraordinary for us, so we, in turn, pay them every month so they will stay. The doctors also work part-time at the main hospital in Abidjan to make some extra money and benefit from valuable on-the-job training. They both petitioned ICMC to sponsor further formal studies at the university, which we were able to do for them.

The clinic's competent, highly respected nurse, Théo, who opened the clinic, has experienced its highs and lows under the most trying circumstances during the past eleven years. The state placed him in Braffouéby back in 2012 and built him a house on the clinic campus, plus another house next to it for one of our midwives. Théo is an important fixture and a true leader.

When the state replaced the original midwife for the very competent Reine, the quality of care improved along with the contributions of another fine nurse, Patrick. The staff has grown and presently consists of two nurses, two midwives, eleven aides, security and maintenance people plus the doctors, and the four or five people in the internship program who often work long hours. ICMC rents a house nearby where the interns live and are paid mainly with food and housing, but most importantly, they learn from our staff. Many of the interns ask to stay after their three-or six-month training. Our goal is to pay them a reasonable salary for their fine work.

More than 50,000 people have been treated at the clinic in the village of Braffouéby, a rural village with a population of just over 1500 people. In 2018 the number of patients receiving care increased by 280%. In 2019 the number increased by another 293%, but during the pandemic in 2020, there was an increase of only 216%. The numbers receiving care began to grow again at the previous pace when the fear of the virus subsided. More space is needed. The dream is to build another maternity clinic and use the original maternity space for the crowded infirmary.

Figure 43 Open-air room built during the pandemic "The Hangar"

Figure 44 Mothers waiting with babies for vaccinations before we built the "hangar"

Figure 45 The Patricia Nau Clinic after installing new awnings

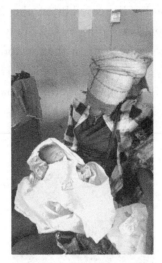

Figure 46 Proud mother with her new baby

Figure 47 The Infirmary side of the clinic

Figure 48 Non-functioning latrines at the school

Most of the schools lack functioning latrines. In the likely case of a young girl finding a leaking pad or a surprise period, the lack of privacy and loss of dignity is devastating and may cause negative psychological effects. For many girls, merely having their monthly period can be the beginning of the end of school because of the social stigma attached to periods and the general lack of safe, sanitary products and inadequate, nonfunctioning communal latrines.

Most believe the discriminating idea that girls having their periods are unclean, and they keep menstruation a taboo topic. If they miss two or three days every month, the girls fall behind and then give up school and get pregnant. Another child would soon be raised in poverty because the mother would be uneducated and unskilled. Many girls never learned basic math or literacy at school.

There is a business plan detailed by Oscar already prepared to build a school in hope of one day having occupational training for young women so that more girls will learn and reach their full potential. If the young girl could have another chance to learn a life skill like farming, raising chickens, or computer training, she could support herself and her children, have hope, self-esteem, and eventually grow out of poverty.

Future Challenges

The village was surrounded by a forest thick with bamboo and different species of palm trees, also mangoes, banana and avocado trees when I lived there, but today the forest is almost completely eliminated, as are many other forests in the country. There have been sparse attempts to replant the trees but not yet in the Sikensi region. The leading causes of deforestation along with major population growth, is from the people who cut the wood not only for cooking but for logging and cocoa production.

It was once predictable when the monsoon rains would come. Nothing is predictable anymore pertaining to climate. There used to be a monsoon season and two "petite rainy seasons" at particular times like clock work. In the last decade, however, there have been numerous floods and severe droughts which harm the fertility of the soil and ruin the crops causing more suffering for the poverty-stricken people.

Young people need jobs to move out of poverty. Training for jobs is necessary, but there must be jobs available. The enormous talent of the young population is wasted because of a lack of opportunity, educational deficits, and poor health as the result of low nutrition, poor sanitation and poverty and corruption. The Sustainable Development Goals (SDG's) aim to eradicate extreme poverty and hunger, malaria and other diseases, promote gender equality, empowerment of women, reduce child mortality and improve maternal health among other lofty targets. Unfortunately, there exists a long-standing resistance to the goal of gender equality and empowerment for women.

In 2023, ICMC was the recipient of one of the SDG's goals, "develop a global partnership for development". In 2021, the World Bank introduced a project called "Financing Based on Performance". Theo and Reine, our nurse and midwife, were rigorously trained in Abidjan alongside other professionals in the region, focusing specifically on improving hygiene and sanitation at the clinics in the region. The training conducted by the World Bank in conjunction with the Ministry of Health was to be passed on and taught to the entire staff to participate in the sponsored program which involved rigid performance standards, strict procedures in sanitation and healthcare practices, and keeping detailed records in collecting data according to their specifications. Following their training, there was a competition among the clinics to evaluate and score their performances.

Our clinic scored the highest when they announced the winners in July, 2023 by delivering a truckload of hospital equipment including new mattresses, ceiling fans, gloves, cleaning supplies, etc., even a privacy screen, air conditioning for the pharmacy, fans for the ceilings, 10 new mattresses, etc.

"This is better than Christmas", exclaimed one of the interns.

The World Bank's goal is to "improve overall sanitation, water, and best practices in the region" and has rewarded other clinics also with supplies also. Every three months the clinics are paid a surprise visit from a representative who grades them. If the clinic continues their improvements, they will receive another generous delivery. They are inspired and committed to continue to improve and remain the best.

The World Bank explained further that through this program, they will also implement comprehensive hygiene education and awareness campaigns to empower individuals with the knowledge and tools necessary for maintaining personal cleanliness and preventing the transmission of diseases.

By affiliating with the World Bank, we gain access to their vast resources, expertise, and global network. In their words, "Our collaboration will enable the World Bank to amplify its impact and execute large-scale projects to improve hygiene and sanitation infrastructure in many of the communities in need. Together we will create lasting change and revolutionize healthcare practices and transform the lives of countless individuals."

I am thrilled with our joint initiative. Their goal of "hygiene and sanitation in schools and public health centers, and access to clean water, appropriate toilets, and adequate waste management systems in institutional setting" will be life-changing. The future looks bright.

Meanwhile...

I am also a grandmother, "Gammy," to my seven "dumplings." Matthew and Amanda's eldest child is Bernard, age 8, an "old soul" who is talented, motivated, and precocious, and his brothers, the inimitable identical twins who love Bernie and everything with wheels, Archer and Winston, 5 years old. Michael and McKenzie have four children, Mary Michael, the very bright and kind sweetheart, age 6, and Julian, known as the diligent, funny, "worker", age 5, the acutely aware, ready for action, Smith K, age 4, and the little precious, playful with attitude, Nancy "Winnie", 2 years. I believe all of them will grow and blossom because of the abundant love and nurturing they receive from their families. If I could be more blessed in my life, I don't know how. I have made peace with my past, and I am doing my best to stay present for a better future for me, my family, and for my Ivorian family.

What I Have Learned

Love your husband or leave him...get on with your life, love your children with everything that you have inside to give, embrace change and be adaptable to new situations. If you are open minded and stay positive you will discover new opportunities for growth. Find something that blows your mind, expands it, and makes you grow even when your struggle fills you with fear, pain and strife ... but make it happen because you know it to be good and true. Come through it on the other side feeling "lucky" because you created it and above all, realize you are blessed. As my dad used to say, "You create your own luck" which meant to "get off your duff and make your dreams come true."

Building a clinic in a poverty-stricken village is not a task that you complete, and then walk away from because disease prevention and treatment is an ongoing challenge. Furthermore, you build friendships more like family who depend on your ability to help support them along the way since their odd jobs and subsistence farming does not pay. The number of people living in extreme poverty in Sikensi region has increased due to its population growth, climate change and corruption which affects every facet of their lives. However, that fact doesn't change the loving and invincible spirit of the Ivorian people, alive and forever optimistic despite the significant obstacles before them.

I have been given an abundance of advantages in my life, and it is clear to me that I took much for granted when I was young and immature. I am deeply grateful for the overwhelming love and generosity from my parents, who offered me every opportunity in life no matter the circumstance. They opened my world and filled it with joy, laughter, music, and shining examples of charity at home and in their community.

I am grateful for my loving family, my cousin, and my friends, and my sons' friends who have all been our very generous support system. I am completely humbled by the fact that so many good people in my life have taken the time to share their energy, wisdom, wit, and encouragement and mostly that they believed in me to change "I can't" to "I did...and still doing it."

If I wrote about how many times I had lost hope, and wallowed in despair, my story would be a sad one. In the early days, I stayed on course and kept the dream alive by having photos of the women and children close to me to remind myself why I could not be defeated. I needed to keep them in mind and their stories alive within me, which were my driving force. When it all felt too overwhelming, I would seek out Kevin or Chas or one of the many kind people who have displayed an interest in our work to talk it out and help find a path to move forward.

I left the Ivory Coast when there was chaos and bloodshed that led to more suffering for the mothers and children, which resulted in more poverty. They had shared their culture with me, and we dreamed about one day creating a better future. It was a futile effort for me to

183

forget Braffouéby and the good chief's goal to build a clinic. He was right. The women needed healthcare and so does everyone else.

We prevailed over the greedy interventions of the bad chief who together with my disloyal friend and the painstakingly slow clinic opening due to their malfeasance. Subsequently, they were faced with the challenge of rebuilding the structure together and the morale. It was a slow transformation, but gratifying.

I never would have thought that we could accomplish so much. People are drinking clean filtered water, children are washing their hands with soap and water in the classrooms and in their homes, and mothers are lining up for prenatal care and with their healthy babies for vaccinations, and post-natal care after delivering their babies in a clean, safe place with professionally trained midwives. Our skilled nurses and midwives have now completely replaced home births and the "traditional" midwives. People are being treated for diseases and illnesses and accidents by competent doctors and nurses in their own village. The sad little girl I knew 23 years ago finished her third year in law school, kids born with Cerebral Palsy are learning to walk with therapy and medications, a young baby boy with a tumor almost as big as his head now has a normal life, a young mother is alive and caring for her children and home after her critical breast surgery, kids have lunches at school, new desks replaced the dilapidated school benches, and heart surgery for a baby boy. We are collaborating with the World Bank! I could go on listing more surgeries and everyday miracles. Our work continues.

Figure 49 Rose with Cerebral Palsy feeling strong and happy

Figure 50 Oscar

Figure 51 New signage thanks to the World Bank

I always admired Oscar because I believed he was the best and the brightest but never thought how fortunate I would be to have someone to work with so capable, having studied math and computer science in college. Besides helping to bring peace and order during the chaotic early years of the clinic with our nurse, Théo, his timely responses as our competent director without fail have inspired me to never lose focus. He answers my questions no matter how mundane or that he has already explained it to me three times, also my endless requests for budgets and vivid written descriptions of needs equipped me with the proper information required to ask everyone I know and don't know for a donation. Without the story to tell, people don't respond.

Oscar now has a side hustle raising organic chickens thanks to the generosity of my cousin, Chas, and a friend I met through J&J's Caring Crowd, John Brennick. Since Oscar is physically unable to perform the tasks himself, he is a "gentleman farmer" with a working organic chicken farm that enables them to sell the birds over Christmas, Ramadan and Easter, the occasions when everyone eats organic chicken. Soon the farm will provide eggs for the malnourished and to those desperately in need of protein-rich foods. The plan is that he divides the profit between the clinic, himself, the farmer and for reinvestment in the business. Oscar is always eager to meet new opportunities to expand his talents. Recently, he has acted as contractor for several buildings, besides his everyday obligations, and has fallen in love.

I salute our dedicated staff who works through the night unlike every other rural clinic in the country. Thank you to all the staff comprised of Oscar, the guard who watches over the property, the departed Osé, who lovingly created the beautiful surrounding flower gardens, shrubbery, and landscaping. Ose's son, Ruben, is our gifted Assistant Director. We commend our doctors, the beloved brothers Kré Felix and Kré Mel, and Theo, our first nurse extraordinaire, nurse Patrick and midwifes Reine and Linda and numerous essential assistive personnel, especially our faithful aides, Emma and Eugénie, and our interns. The team has provided better health in the region by making it more accessible and for giving quality, dedicated care.

The Ministry of Health called the Patricia Nau clinic "the bulldozer" because it "keeps on going no matter the challenge." They broke the mold of an Ivorian rural clinic because of the pharmacy, laboratory, incinerator, a person charged with sanitation, and most importantly, the outstanding staff with grit.

The efforts by the World Bank help our non-profit in the USA because we are now able to focus our fundraising on the salaries of the hard-working, underpaid staff and for those very sick patients, especially in need of our aid for medicine, vaccinations or transfers to a hospital where care would be unattainable for people living in extreme poverty. And, of course, we don't forget the orphaned children and the kind people caring for them.

Like the sturdy branches of an old oak, my spirit thrives as my roots are nourished by the love of my cherished family and friends. I am filled with profound gratitude and appreciation for the abundant love, kindness and compassion that surrounds me which brings an unshak-able joy to my deepest core.

One day while visiting Braffouéby, I took a photo of a young boy wearing a red t-shirt (and nothing else) with the refrain, "All You Need Is Love," which, to me and the Beatles, says it all. Thank you for helping us show the love.

Figure 52 Love

Thank you for purchasing this book and reading about our story.

All funds go directly to the clinic and projects of Ivory Coast Mothers and Children.

You are invited to help continue our work and show the love by donating to

www.IvoryCoastAid.org

About the Author

 Patricia, a divorced mother of two sons, and one of six siblings has had a life filled with diverse experiences. After joining the Peace Corps at age 56, she served in the Ivory Coast and Kenya. She started a non-profit organization in 2008. Through this organization, Patricia has been raising funds for the clinic, clean water, orphan support, scholarships, and emergency response in an impoverished community. Her resilience and determination are evident as she actively works to make a meaningful impact on the lives of others.